The Backward Sex

Other titles in the New Zealand Classics series

The Backward Sex

Ian Cross

OXFORD UNIVERSITY PRESS

Auckland   Melbourne   Oxford   New York

Oxford University Press

Oxford   New York   Toronto
Delhi   Bombay   Calcutta   Madras   Karachi
Petaling Jaya   Singapore   Hong Kong   Tokyo
Nairobi   Dar es Salaam   Cape Town
Melbourne   Auckland
and associated companies in
Beirut   Berlin   Ibadan   Nicosia

Oxford is a trade mark of Oxford University Press

First published 1960
Reprinted as a New Zealand Classic 1987
© Ian Cross 1960
This edition © Ian Cross 1987

ISBN 0 19 558172 5

Cover designed by John McNulty
Printed in Hong Kong
Published by Oxford University Press
5 Ramsgate Street, Auckland, New Zealand

TO BARNEY

1

My best friend, Harry Maddox, put his arms around my waist and kissed me on the cheek after my father's funeral. We were just twelve years old.

'That's the stupidest thing a chap can do,' he said, 'but I had to show you somehow.'

He was on the verge of tears.

At my father's funeral the men carrying his coffin struggled to hold their footing on the muddy slope of the slight incline leading to the grave. They were fearful, as if they were about to drop their burden over the edge of an abyss and were in danger of falling with it. When they lowered the coffin, there was a splash of water; it had rained very hard the night before.

Harry is the best, the very best in Albertville. When we were eight, we played truant from the Albertville East Primary School to celebrate the discovery that our birthdays were on the same day, that day. We walked a mile to the patch of trees on the boundary of the town park, and during the afternoon collected six thrush eggs, found one dead blackbird, and were frightened by a swooping magpie with a clicking beak. Bettsy Horner, who was two years older than anybody else in the class, told on us and the teacher kept us in after school for the next two days. We were never sure how Bettsy found out, but Harry hit her twice in the body and sat on her, he was so angry. She was a different girl after that.

Most of Albertville is on the north bank of the river. This river drifts into the sea, and hills on each side of the town hump back into plateaux of good farmland. The real money in Albertville is farm money, but that goes for the rest of New Zealand, too. Even now there are not many more than 20,000 people living in Albertville, so I'm not exactly a big city boy. I was a boy running a trolley downhill into Victoria Avenue on a Monday afternoon, and Victoria Avenue is the main street, although, to be quite fair, my trolley run was north of the shopping area, and care was needed. Between Albertville and the sea is a strip of untidy dairy land, swamp near the river, sandy away from it, to the north, carrying cows with piebald udders, boxthorn hedges, rickety milk-stands, salt-stained houses, gates of chicken-netting stapled to loose battens, slack-wired fences, and grass so green and so strong in the spring that it clumps and mats in the uneaten places. At the river mouth is Raggleton, a grubby little place around the freezing works and a pub, with a wharf and a dredge that has to work hard to keep a depth to the channel for the lighters that carry the meat and wool out to the ships in the roadstead.

Harry and I were especially fond of the Crown land at the back of the town, upriver, no more than twenty minutes' walk from the boundary. We liked to shoot there, and we both knew the fascination of watching a live thing twitching to death. We liked this land torn about by small creeks that were powdered silt in the summer and muddy little torrents in the winter; a mixture of flax, thistles, manuka scrub and blackberry patches covered most of it, but there were licks of flat country with a wire-rooted brown stuff that passed for grass. This place offered the rabbits a refuge from the farmers after they had fed off the good plateau land, and we made it that much less of a refuge with an old .22 we owned on a fifty-fifty basis, shooting in turn, and quickly, because there was so much cover; we wounded and lost as many rabbits as we killed, although we always aimed for the head or shoulder. A lot of people went shooting there, and in our time it was noticeable that the rabbits were pulling back upriver, and sometimes we went two or three miles, some of the distance in fairly rough going, without getting a shot. There were more than enough mighty hunters for the little bunnies.

A rabbit dies gently, although not with the same reproach as a deer, as I have since discovered. A deer has a rather nasty habit of living until the moment of your arrival and gazing at you with liquid brown eyes full of sorrow, and then dying with a twinge of breath that is too damn much like a sigh. A rabbit quivers and kicks, quite gently, and never tries to establish such embarrassing contact. We would kill a wounded rabbit by lifting it up by the hind legs and slapping hard down on its neck with the heel of a hand; but occasionally we took no such action and watched a death spasm, wondering.

'Could you do that to a human being?' Harry asked me once.

'No,' I said. 'I think I could shoot at a man, but I would be careful not to hit him.'

'If I was actually going to shoot, I think I would have to hit what I was shooting at,' said Harry, and I remembered that.

This was the last year of the war, so the conversation was not unnatural, there being so much talk of killing human beings in the last few years. But I laughed at

Harry and doubted then whether he could ever point a gun at anybody.

'I'll show you sometime,' he said, frowning.

I knew that I should not have kidded Harry: he was always one for action and I always had to strive to keep up with him: the Bettsy Horner business I had matched by climbing over somebody's fence and stealing strawberries, which I detested, merely because Harry wanted some. From that time on, it was understood that we would do each other's dirty or tough work. This arrangement gained us considerable distinction over the years, and in our final year at primary school I had six fights against kids with whom I had no personal quarrel, while Harry looked on with satisfied belligerence. The fact that I had involved him in only one fight in return for my six this year worried him, though, and to make up for it he met my appointment for a dental check-up. A year I had to have three teeth out. Harry, thank goodness, lost that quarrelsome streak when we went on to high school, and the only really tricky task I had to perform for him was to toss a rotten egg at Gummy Saunders, the English teacher, who had never liked Harry, and one day made several sarcastic remarks to the whole class about an essay which he kept referring to as 'this piece of Maddox madness'.

'He's got to be hit with a rotten egg,' Harry said afterwards. 'I'm sorry, Robert, old chap.'

'Don't mention it,' I said, and the next week during a lunch-hour, hit Gummy in the chest with the egg as he came out of the main building. This egg was dropped from a top floor window. There was a rumpus about it all, but nobody suspected me, and Harry had his alibi. Actually, I rather liked Gummy.

10

This same year Harry performed what he chose to regard as an outstanding piece of dirty work for me. It was, too. This year Palmerston North High School had in their forwards a Samoan, a big chap with fuzzy hair, concrete bones under thick black skin, and a huge smile for everybody he bashed into the ground. In the second half of the game against us he smashed through a line-out, and, as full-back, I had to wait for him in pained expectation as he charged, head down, knees and elbows like swinging war clubs, a half-a-ton of weight behind each swing. I had braced myself and bent down for the tackle, knowing I didn't have a chance, when I heard a collision of flesh and bone, and the snap of a breaking bone. Harry had cut across from his wing and taken the tackle. This Samoan came down with a crash that literally jarred the ground underneath the sprigs of my boots; the ball rolled loose and I was able to clear. Harry had a broken collar-bone. It was part of our deal, of course.

The incident with the gun was not a piece of dirty work, but it did involve a matching of accomplishment once Harry had felt the niggle of my challenge.

A few weeks later, when we were out with the .22 again, we sighted an elderly man fossicking about the edge of the Crown land, not far from the dead end of the road from town. The wrinkles of the old man's neck extended half-way up his bald head.

'Watch this,' said Harry, fingering a bullet in the gun. He worked around through a patch of high grass and trees, breaking into the open nearly a hundred yards away, directly behind the man. He stood there, in a dapple of sunlight and shadow, the gun raised and pointed at the man's back, his finger on the trigger. It seemed a very long time before he lowered the rifle and ducked back into the trees, so long that I nearly yelled out; my upset must have been visible, for when he got back he said, 'I don't hear you laughing now.'

An hour later, on our way back to the road without even seeing a rabbit, he was still harping on what he had done; he was elated, and full of kick, having collected a grain of experience that he could not share with me, even if he wanted to. So when we came upon this old chap again, squatting by the pile of firewood he had collected, his back to us, pipe-smoke curling over his shoulder, I hissed to Harry to be quiet and took the gun from him. The gun was loaded, and I made a great show of unsnipping the safety catch. Then I moved back and around beside a clump of stunted manuka, dropped to my stomach and took a sight on that bald head, like an over-size tennis ball, the worse for much wear. My heart was beating raw against the ground and my breath was tangling in my throat, but I had enough sense left to realise that it would be better if this old chap did not actually hear the bullet zing past, and I shifted the gun a little higher than I had first intended and twisted my body away in a scrambling circle at the instant of firing. When this old chap jumped to his feet I was on my knees, now facing towards the river, away from him, the gun pointed in the same direction. He didn't seem to have much sense in his face; he made a vague gesture with his pipe and that was that. He had every right to extreme perturbation, but there he was, merely startled, and I wondered whether I should have put the bullet nearer his dumb head.

Harry crooked his arm around my neck as we walked away and exclaimed, 'You bloody beaut, Henderson.' I was generous enough to allow that his keeping the gun sighted on the man for so long quite matched my own action. It was not without satisfaction, however, that I noticed that he was not sure about this, and occasionally raised the gun to his shoulder and clicked the trigger on the empty magazine.

2

Harry and I never thought much about girls, except as fellow human beings. We sometimes discussed them in an abstract kind of way, always more or less in their favour. Our contact with their sex was, by our own choice, limited, although Harry had once indulged in what he described as 'excursions into the realms of anatomical knowledge'. These came to an abrupt halt in our second year at high school, which was co-educational, when he and a girl named Thea Thoms drifted away from an open-air botany lecture at Kitchener Park and disappeared into a huge clump of hydrangeas. He never told me the whole story, but apparently he had been fairly startled in the hydrangeas and when, a year later, Thea was expelled for following Scrooge Miller, the Latin master, into the cloakroom and making an astounding suggestion, Harry nodded his head and said he thought so. I was glad that Harry had lost this early interest in girls.

Albertville High School was a conglomeration of brick permanence and prefabrication. There was the Old Building of red brick that had been faded to a light orange by the sun; it carried a modest amount of ivy on its two-storeys – almost enough to hide the crack made by the earthquake of 1930. Behind this was the original woodwork and engineering block, a neat little box of ageing wood, with small sash windows of milky glass that filtered light with understandable reluctance on to the benches and the first products of schoolboy tradesmen. Across a tarsealed yard was the New Wing, equal parts plywood, gibralter board, tin and glass, melded to a light steel frame, the whole thing looking like a well-arranged scrap-heap. There was a sprinkling of minor buildings, too, and tennis courts and swimming baths, and a wide expanse of playing field behind. Across the road was a rambling old house, a sort of Gothic monstrosity in wood, taken over many years ago for the girls. The school was co-educational up to a point: the girls and boys shared many of the same classes, but that was about all. Anyway, the boys called the house across the street Bloomer Castle, and were never much interested in it.

So it was that when one Saturday afternoon Harry and I strolled over to the tennis club, which was run by the Old Pupils' Association on the school courts, I was astounded when Harry became entangled with a girl named Jillian, who tied her blonde hair back off her round head with an unnecessarily large red ribbon, and swished her skirt around so much on the courts that her panties, shaped rather like jockey underwear, showed at least twice. I tried to get him back on the rails, without any success, and found myself stuck with Jillian's friend, Margery, a girl with an aloof manner and wide hips.

'Look,' I said, when Harry and Jillian came laughing off the courts after a game of singles. 'What about giving these girls a game of doubles? You and I against the pair of them.'

'A great idea,' cried Harry, already raddled by the sun. 'Only let's mix it up, Roberto. Jillian and I against you and her friend, eh?' He grinned and called to Jillian. 'What about that, oh blonde one? Partner up with old Harry Maddox, a future Wimbledon champion, for a game of mixed doubles.'

Jillian swished right around, her baby face full of giggles, and said, 'Yes, please,' and slapped her racquet gently against Harry's shoulder. He uttered an absurd squeak, as though he was thrilled to very little pieces, and spent the rest of the hot afternoon skittering and yelling around the girl, making an extraordinary fool of himself, while Margery, who was shaped rather like a triangle, looked on in amazement. I was amazed too, and wanted to sling him over the high wire netting about those asphalt courts.

When it was all over, Harry gave Jillian a ride home on the bar of his bicycle, as though he had been doing that kind of thing all of his life, and I was faced with the nervous effort of avoiding any responsibility for escorting Margery home. However, this girl seemed as dismayed as I was by the whole performance, and the solemn dignity with which she disappeared, without any bother, made me feel quite grateful to her.

All the next week I was stewing with resentment over the fact that Harry should be so damned handsome: he was dark, broad-shouldered, thin-hipped and long-legged, his blue eyes glittered like a bad boy's most of the time, and his smile had a lot of white teeth in it; he was in a constant simmer of the joy of living, and unaware that the cut and balance of his strong features (especially the slant of his cheek-bones and eyes) made him good to look at. Fair-haired, my eyes a treacle brown, as tall as Harry, and as strong, I did not have quite the same width of shoulder, and unfortunately the tilt of my nose, the dimples of my

15

cheeks, the smoothness and shape of my mouth and the yellow-wisp mess of my hair all combined to suggest an over-grown pixie, and naturally I resented this, and had already taken scissors and clipped my eye-lashes back, wanting to be more firm in appearance. Now I was troubled by the pimples erupting around the line of my jaw: all this week I drank a yeast compound mixture three times a day, applied hot and cold flannels to my face behind a locked bathroom door, and also consumed gallons of water. The one good thing about pimples, I said to myself as I forced each glass of water into my squelching body, was that they kept giggling girls out of a chap's hair.

The following Friday, after a week during which we had not touched the subject, Harry was pleased as we walked home after school, and I knew what was coming.

'I won't be able to go to the pictures or anything like that as usual tonight, Roberto,' he said. 'It's Jillian again – I'm taking her out. There's nothing like a girl.'

'That's all right. I've always got plenty to do.'

Harry swaggered his wide shoulders about, looking bloody pleased, the skin of his face as clear as a baby's bottom. 'You ought to get a girl,' he said. 'It's not bad, I tell you.'

'No thank you.'

'She kisses like nobody's business, Jillian, at the gate. I didn't get home till midnight when I took her out on Wednesday.'

'All right, all right, I don't want to hear.'

'It is time, old Roberto, for you to get a girl, I tell you.'

'Where do you get this "I tell you, I tell you" stuff?'

'I get that from Jillian,' Harry said. 'Everything she says she finishes off by saying, "I tell you".'

'Sounds stupid to me.'

'Fat lot you know about girls, I tell you.'

'You sound just like a stupid girl.'

Harry stopped. 'Well, keep your hair on,' he said. 'I'm cutting off here. Be seeing you.' He turned off down Victoria Avenue, in the opposite direction to where he lived. And just when I was about to call after him, he got in first by crying over his shoulder, 'You've got a lot to learn, I tell you.' He emphasized the last three words, the bastard.

3

My step-mother said to me, 'And what's bothering you?'

'Nothing,' I said, and nagged her about getting tea ready on time: if I wasn't careful, she'd let it drift on until about eight o'clock. The slippers were crumbling off her feet, her stockings were laddered and sagging in the usual slack wrinkles about her ankles. How somebody with the gentlemanly elegance of my father came to marry her still perplexed me, although I was very fond of her; she was the only mother I had ever known, my real mother having died not long after I was born. Careless, imprecise and happy, she gave the impression she was not quite ready for whatever was happening to her or whatever she had to be doing: sometimes she was just above five minutes away from preparedness, other times she was hours, even days away. Her cheeks were ruddy and inflated, and her forehead and chin, even her nose, had something of

17

the same smooth roundness, and so her mouth and eyes were set in the clefts of joining bulges. Her grey hair was nearly always in curlers and under a net, and on the rare occasions it did emerge was groomed into rather thin wriggles. The twinkle of her eyes was emphasized by some radiance of good humour in her face, which was pleasant, even genuinely comic, I suppose. At one time, I had been a little ashamed of her faint brogue, but I felt I had outgrown that and was a good son to her, and from an early age prompted her about things that had to be done about the house and helped with the two bed-and-breakfast guests we had kept since my father's final illness. On winter nights before the fire, after she had a couple of gins (I knew about this early, and didn't mind) she would produce a battered little concertina and squeeze these confounded little Irish songs out of it, her head to one side, the shine of the fire reflecting on the dampness of her cheeks. I was really quite fond of her. Whenever I could save enough money I'd buy her something to encourage her to keep up to scratch. But now, waiting for my tea, I was sour about her appearance, and though she laughed at all this grumpiness, the happy-go-lucky treatment wasn't working this time.

After tea I was still sour – but about Albertville now, a town which hitherto had seemed a peaceful little paradise, uncrowded and unbustled, the best place in the world to live in. Now I was sour on the place, that was all, and saw it for what it was, a small corner of a small country of grassland fenced by batten and wire, sheep shorn naked (this was the summer time), cows chewing, wooden towns with nearly every building under the wrinkle of corrugated iron, and so much grass everywhere that there was scarcely any room for trees. Standing in the centre of my bedroom, the tidiest room in the whole house, wondering how on earth I could bear to live in such a country, I thumped a clenched fist against my thigh, grabbed a pillow from my bed, drop-kicked it against the large frame windows, and thought of the fool I had been in not giving Harry Maddox a black eye for his confounded cheek; you don't get honey by tickling a bee's arse.

Then came this inspiration. 'You stinking drain,' I told myself, as I stood in the hall and flicked over the pages of the telephone book and found what I wanted: Jillian's address. Back in the bedroom, sitting at the table under the window, the blinds down, the door locked, I began to compose a letter to Jillian's father. The style was to be quite formal:

Mr James Fairchild
89 Delhi Crescent
ALBERTVILLE
Dear Sir,

I think you should know more about your daughter Jillian and her association with a boy. Do you know she is . . .

It was here that my letter bogged down. How exactly could I describe Jillian's actions? I chewed the end of my fountain pen, studied the brown wallpaper and then got up and swished a cricket bat around to help me think – and thought of her bouncing around on the tennis courts, being in the middle of everything, swishing her skirts around to let everybody know she was something of a dancer, and then twisting Harry around her little finger like that. I remembered Harry saying that he had not got home from the pictures until midnight: with the theatre finishing at 10.45 p.m., and only

19

a twenty-minute walk to her place, this meant that she and Harry must have been messing around at the gate for another twenty minutes, allowing Harry half-an-hour to get back to his own place by midnight.

My first impulse was to use the word 'cheap' to describe her, but as soon as this word was on paper I saw her giggle-bright face and was ashamed, and didn't want to be nasty about the girl; really, it was for her own sake, in a way, that the letter was being written; at her age it would be a favour to be saved from heading in the wrong direction. So I screwed up my first attempt and started again, this time borrowing from a court report in the *Herald,* the words, 'carnal inducement'. But I considered the report, which was about a business man who embezzled just about all his firm's money to spend on some woman with a bad name in Wellington, and decided that Jillian very likely had a good name, and was not sending Harry off his rocker. She was using inducements, of course, but I became uneasy about the word carnal, and decided that her father might not know exactly what it meant.

So it was at my third attempt, after chewing my knuckles for a while, that I settled the issue. 'Dear Sir,' I wrote, 'I think you should know more about your daughter Jillian, and her association with a boy. Do you realise she is using unladylike tactics of behaviour?' After a little more thought I signed the letter, 'Well-wisher', addressed it carefully, put it in my hip pocket, and set out for a walk, intending to find a letter-box on the way.

'Dear me, you do look worried,' Miss Rookes blithered when I met her at the gate on the way out. She paid three pounds a week and liked a full pot of tea in the morning. I grunted a few words about being thoughtful, that was all, and pressed on, in no mood for the old dear.

4

Something of a coward, I didn't hurry about posting this letter, and drifted to the far side of the town, to the slopes of Trig Hill, and sat there. It was a good place to take a depression, I supposed, for Albertville did have a decent setting: the green of the plateau slopes carried deeper greens in patches of native bush and trees, livened by seasonal smacks of yellow and gold; the river did loop the town with peace and a sort of purity, here and there exposing a cliff-face eroded and shaped by weather and water into permanent character; there was still a fresh memory of the wilderness mystery beyond the Crown land; the air was always clean, and most times carried the sight and sound of sky life, even if it was no more than the flit and chirp of the smaller birds. I could see the valley sliding towards the sea, where the sky loomed so big and high as it flamed overhead in the setting sun that the whole blessed universe might have been catching fire. Sounds drifted above the town, no more than casual echoes, the smell of the sea was in the slow stirring of the breeze from the west, and the earth was warm to my backside. It all merely made my depression sentimental, but this was an improvement.

I drifted down towards the houses and street lights of Ellis Street, near the foot of the hill, and was full of thoughts of how in the middle of each light were people, talking and being together, while I was alone and outside. There was no light for me as I mooned along past the shadowy neatness of the houses, with their front lawns hedged from the footpath. Above a garage that edged right on to the line of the footpath a voice called, 'Hello, there.' This voice was hesitant and small, and almost drowned by the fuss of starlings settling down in macrocarpa trees back up the hill. At first I thought it was no more than a voice carried a distance and made audible by a flick of the breeze. Then again it came, 'Up here,' and above me a shape was sticking out over the edge of a garage.

'Oh . . . hello,' I said.

The shape pulled back, there was a scuffling on the roof. The garage wasn't much bigger than a little Austin, and it belonged to a house that looked as though it was the home of the driver and no more than two passengers. But it was a new house, made of creosoted timber, with a flat roof, and white weather-boarding, all quite impressive just after the end of the war, when new houses were a novelty. Anyway, this shape clattered about on the garage roof and, by moving forward slightly, I saw it climb down a ladder at the side of the garage. It was this triangular girl, Margery somebody or other.

'I didn't recognise you at first,' I said.

She leaned over the gate, no more than a couple of feet from my chin, as though we were friends, instead of people who just belonged to the same tennis club.

'I watched you mooching up the street, but I didn't know it was you until you were right underneath.'

'That's a pretty funny place for you to be, up there, at your age.'

'I'm sixteen and expect I'll sit up there when I feel like it till I'm quite old,' she said.

I kicked my foot into the asphalt, helpless for some reason: the girl seemed talkative and certainly quite different from what she had been at the tennis club. I wished I'd said hello, and kept on going.

'What's so good about sitting on the roof of a garage?' I asked.

She fixed her elbows on top of the gate, fanned both hands out and waggled them vaguely.

'Don't you ever feel . . . well, I don't know. Sometimes there's nothing else a person can do.'

'Girls always have plenty to do, don't they?' I think I was scratching the top of my chest now. 'Boys I can understand sitting on a roof, but girls . . .' I stopped scratching and flipped my hand back and forward in the air before I realised that I was imitating her waggles.

'Are you going somewhere?' she asked.

'No. I'm walking. Getting exercise, that is.'

'Call that walking – you were moving like a snail.'

'Well, it doesn't do to go flat out all the time. Fast, then slow, and so on.'

I was about to say, 'Well, nice to have seen you,' and walk on, when she headed me off by saying, 'It's funny, my talking to you like this.'

'Is it? I mean I don't think so,' I said, slightly miffed: what was so funny about talking to me?

'It's just that it is a feeling I get, sometimes. I get very talkative sometimes and when I saw you walking along like that I really got the feeling. You know why?'

'No.'

'I thought you looked like me. Not really like me, but your walking like that, so slow, is a lot like sitting on the roof of a garage if you ask me.'

'Nobody asked you.'

The plain fact was that this girl had caught me absolutely pulpy and defenceless: only the doubtful light protected me. She was not a great deal more than a shape, even now: her features were discernible, but I did not like to make a full appraisal of her, although I noted that her hair was pulled back behind her head and tied into a knot, that she was wearing a sleeveless dress, and her arms and shoulders as she leaned forward were quite clearly a girl's arms and shoulders. Her face was pretty enough, as I remembered from tennis, but it wasn't possible to study it without running slap into her eyes. The evening began to feel far too warm, almost suffocating.

'Don't be offended. I'm not insulting you,' she was saying. 'In fact, I'm going to tell you something. I sit up on the garage when I'm lonely, and sitting up there makes it official.'

'Lonely?' I said. 'A girl lonely? Why don't you go out to the pictures with a girlfriend – or a boyfriend, for that matter? Girls always have plenty to do.'

I was looking directly into her eyes, so surprised at what she had said.

'I'll be frank with you, Robert,' she said. 'I'm too broad around the beam.'

'What do you mean? I don't know what you mean,' I said, folding my arms over my chest, to see if that helped.

'My hips, silly. Nobody looks at a girl with wide hips. I've got wide hips.'

I was about to say, 'You funny thing,' but checked myself in time, and then said, 'What's that got to do with the price of fish?'

'I don't know. I feel out of it, that's all.'

24

She straightened back from the gate and looked at her hands as though she was considering her own words and losing her confidence.

'I don't see what you have to worry about,' I said. 'Look, I have a bad case of pimples. It doesn't worry me. I would rather be . . . be broad, and I'm not saying you are broad, but I would rather be, than have these pimples. But it doesn't worry me a bit. No sir.'

'Pimples are nothing. Lots of boys have pimples. They're nothing.'

'What do you mean, nothing? They are a whole lot. They can spoil everything. They can——'

'They do worry you then.'

'Insofar as my appearances. You have to have regard for appearances.'

'I think your appearances are fine. I don't see what you have to worry about. Pimples are nothing.'

'Well, a girl wouldn't understand. Nobody would . . . You know, I've never thought your . . . your whatever you call them – your proportions, that is. I can't see anything wrong there. Not everybody likes these skinny girls. It's healthy, very healthy, I dare say, not being skinny. And you're growing more upward. You might say it is too early to tell exactly how you will turn out. It certainly is very silly of you to sit up on a roof about it.'

'Just as silly as you roaming about the streets like a snail.'

'Look, it is not the same. Two different things entirely.'

Even in the bad light I saw – or did I guess? – that she was disappointed at this remark, so I added, 'But I can see what you mean, though. It is a very intelligent observation, although not necessarily right. But

25

very sensible when I think about it. Not many people talk intelligently.'

'Thank you.'

'That's all right. And I can't see that you should feel out of anything. And you're a good tennis player, too.'

She was suddenly quiet, and because her eyes were out of my way, I could peer hard at her face, and be reminded that she was very nice, in an Italian kind of way, or any place where the girls had dark hair, for that matter.

'Well, I'll get along now. I'm keeping you out in the dark.'

'Oh, no – I like it in the dark.'

'It certainly gets dark, doesn't it?'

'It does.'

Back inside the house a door closed. I stood back from the gate and shoved my hand into my hip-pocket and fingered this letter I'd written to Jillian's father. It was smooth and cold and for some reason reminded me of the razor blade I used at school as a pencil sharpener.

'I'll be getting along,' I said.

'Where are you going?' A lot of the fizz had gone out of her voice.

'I don't know where I was going, but anyway I'm not going there now,' I said. 'I'll go back home I suppose. I'm not sure.'

'Oh.'

We were isolated in a difficult silence. Albertville was always quiet at night, except for the occasional rumble of a tram.

'Where are you going to now?' I felt compelled to ask.

'I'll read, I think.'

'I just thought,' I said, still under the same glorious compulsion, ' – I just thought that if you happened to be going somewhere on my way I wouldn't mind walking with you, that's all.'

'I wish I was, but I'm not.'

'Well, I'm on my way then. I'll see you at tennis, I suppose.'

'Yes, I'm going tomorrow afternoon.'

'That's funny. So am I. I thought about two o'clock.'

'That's the same time I'll be going.'

Her voice was so low, so lacking in confidence, that it made me feel very brave indeed. 'Well,' I said. 'If we're going about the same time, I might as well drop by – I mean it is practically on my way, really. I'll walk over with you.'

'That is very nice of you if you would. I would. That is, I would wait for you if you were late and' – she had some of that fizz back – 'and if you are early, I'll be ready early just in case.'

That was it, of course. I bubbled my way back home, feeling twinges of hallucinatory belief that it was possible to leap up and brush my hand across the dark sky, or call out and be heard by every happy person on earth. I actually held out my arms like a little boy playing at aeroplanes, and zoomed around the corner of Hobson Street, towards home, emitting a loud hissing noise.

Harry Maddox was waiting for me, sitting on the tin fence of our place, heel-hammering, hand-flapping, husking out sounds with jerking head, probably dreaming that he was drumming with Bunny Rexall's Pacific Hot Shots at the Kiwi Kabaret. Bunny was very hot on drums, according to local judges, who didn't know the half of it.

'What the hell are you doing here?' I asked Harry.

'I'm waiting for you, Roberto. Your mother thought you would be back.'

I rubbed a hand over the outline of the letter in my hip pocket. This hand hurt.

'I've been out, talking to Margery – you know, that friend of Jillian's.'

'Gee, Margery. You. She's a genius.'

'What's that again?'

'A genius, according to Jillian. Got an I.Q. way the dickens up there. And you taking on with her. You know she can play the piano, the violin, and sings, along with all this intelligence.'

'Well, I certainly find her conversation pleasant. Yes, I can see that she might be intelligent. I can see that.'

He pushed my shoulder, laughing. 'I might have known. You two quiz kids. Fancy you, though. Her being able to play all that music, and singing, that's something.'

'As a matter of fact——' I paused, to make sure of being casual, ' – I'm taking her out to tennis tomorrow afternoon.'

'Well, I'll be darned. But what about tonight? Let's walk around the great metropolis.'

'What happened to Jillian?'

'Her?' Harry snapped his fingers. 'She's had tooth-ache, and her mother won't let her come out. Not that I worry. Next week I'm taking that Monica Hickson out; you know, that dark girl in the same street as our place. I don't know anything about dark girls – but come on, let's get mobile.'

But there was something that had to be done first. In this great big night, in this peaceful little paradise, so uncrowded and unbustled, the best place in the world to live in, I trotted down the path (the trellis gate floated open underneath my hand), made my way around the house and went to the rubbish incinerator and the light from the kitchen window made this old drum look beautiful. Reaching into my hip pocket I took out the letter and was actually tearing it into shreds over the black mouth of the drum, into the smell of the rusty burnings of years, before Harry knew exactly what was happening.

'What the hell is going on?' he asked, jostling against me.

'Incriminating document,' I replied. 'All agents read and destroy.' I crumpled the last few pieces of paper together and plunged my hands half-way down into the drum, stirring up the powdery mess.

'It must be a red-hot love letter,' said Harry.

'Something like that,' I said.

Back on the footpath, after I had been inside to wash my hands, Harry said, 'That Margery girl. I bet with her intelligence she could play boogie woogie and swing, along with all this high-brow stuff. I'll get Monica or Jillian or somebody, and all four of us will do things. We might as well concentrate on girls together, seeing we've done everything else together, eh?'

I was warm because the night was warm, and I was warm because of something else again.

'Righto, but first things first,' I said. 'About tonight. I know you don't like Shakespeare, but we will go to the pictures and see that old Romeo and Juliet, or it will be too bad for you, boy.'

Harry halted and buried his face in his hands, posing under the street light. 'That's what I get for associating with intellectuals,' he moaned, and then flung his hands screeching skyward. There was nothing tremendously funny in his action but I laughed my eyes wet. There was going to be no more trouble over the opposite sex for me, so I thought.

5

I had a wonderful winter with Margery, and Harry had a wonderful winter with one girl after another. There was only one worry for me, and nobody guessed it, not even Bunny Rexall. Margery and I were at this school dance together, and Bunny came over and tossed charm around like great gobs of treacle: Bunny always went out of his way to be pleasant to her. This dance was in the school assembly hall; the floor was waxed and french chalk was strewn over it like a snowfall; chairs were lined against three walls and on each side of the stage. With the paper streamers on the ceiling, the school motto on a huge placard suspended by wire over the stage, and with the chaps in their sports clothes or suits and the girls in pretty decent dresses, the whole show seemed a grand affair indeed. The band, of course, was Bunny Rexall and His Hot Shots. Bunny was a thin little man with black hair that looked so much like patent leather that it might have been tended with a shoe-brush and polish. His band played for most of the dances in Albertville and sometimes Harry filled in for him on the drums (Harry could make them sound like the poundings of his own excited heart). It was at supper-time that Bunny swarmed all over Margery: with his moustache about half the length of his upper lip, his blue button eyes, his sharp-creased grey slacks and blazer with gold buttons, he

30

made a considerable impression; it pleased her that I was acquainted with a local celebrity.

Later, trough-to-trough with him in the cloakroom, he said to me, 'I see you're a man now, Robert.' I knew he was thinking of Margery.

'I suppose I am, just about,' I said.

Bunny stepped back, and said, 'I bet there's nothing much you don't know.'

I suppose I giggled. I'm not sure.

'We'll compare notes sometime,' he said.

He was paying me some kind of tribute, and I was pleased that the cause of my worry was not apparent to a shrewd man like Bunny Rexall, who must be over thirty years of age.

The fact was that I was ashamed that the things Margery and I enjoyed doing together were so friendly. There was nothing more typical of our friendship than that we both liked going to the lip of the southern plateau and sensing the tremendous significance of the view.

'There are nearly 20,000 people living about Albertville,' I said one blustery Sunday afternoon, 'and we are the only two who know how wonderful it is up here.'

A high wind, salt-hard from the sea, was stinging tears to our eyes, numbing our ears: we had to hunch our shoulders and cradle our bodies with our arms.

'Yes,' she shouted. 'It makes me awfully pleased I am alive.'

On the left was the sea, which filled to a swollen depth where the plateau dropped away sharply, or could only be glimpsed as a faint line where the plateau maintained its height for many miles before collapsing to the shore line. The strength of the sea

31

can always be felt on an island, even such a large one as the North Island: it tangs the air and the wind, and makes the rivers an intimate link with the land it embraces.

On the other side of the road there was a view of the strength opposing the sea, and it seemed that the road ran across the point of stability between the two forces. The ridges on the right were tough sinews, indicating that there was more to this land than the green fat of farms. On a clear day, the horizon pulled back and this other strength became naked: the ridges were seen to be foothills of ranges that rolled like tidal waves of earth towards the centre of the island, where they converged and shaped huge mountains that hit the sky hard.

We often cycled from Albertville to the top of this plateau on Sundays, during the winter, even though it was fairly hard going (we had to walk with our bicycles up the steeper grades). On the way back it was easy, of course, coasting downhill all the way to the floor of the river valley, where the road swung through a patch of bush and came upon the Albert River, as though it was making an unexpected discovery. Other Sundays we would walk along the northern river bank, past the willow trees dripping into the water to where marram grass, lupine and manuka tangled about lonely foot tracks. Or we would stroll about the town, agreeing that Albertville was a little decadent, and that the two lines of tram tracks that rutted the centre of Victoria Avenue were a disgrace, and that only the sprinkling of three-storey buildings made the shopping centre look anything at all; that it was a pity that the lesser shops, built early in the century, should hide the decaying rear of their premises with elaborate fronts that fooled nobody, and that the only real signs of hope were in the new buildings : the post office, a picture theatre, a hotel, the Bank of New Zealand, and the library, which was visible up a sidestreet on the crest of a small hill. There was certainly little to look at and be pleased in the whole town : the paint was flaking on house walls and corrugated iron roofs, only a few trees lined the streets, that too often looked as though they had nowhere to go. There was no town hall, and the road bridge that spanned the Albert River was an ancient inadequacy that the town had been thinking of replacing for a quarter of a century. The seats of our trams were hard wooden slats, and the lines of the tram tracks were pot-holed and rutted. It must have been that the beauty of this town's setting daunted the first settlers of a hundred years before, and the belief had arisen that people did not have to create beauty when there was so much around them already.

On wet Sundays I would go around to Margery's place in the afternoon and play chess.

'It's the old story. You get a couple of insignificant pawns up on me, then proceed to swap like nobody's business,' I said once, annoyed at what were obviously unfair tactics against a man who liked to build up a terrific attack and then cut loose and mop up his opponent as the reward for the crafty disposition of his forces. She could often frustrate this by exchanging pieces early, ruining everything.

'I can play what game I like, so long as I conform to the rules.' She beamed back into the face of what I hoped was my stern stare. 'I get nervous watching you wrinkling your head, not just your brow but your whole blessed head, over the board, and making these mysterious moves that are awfully important in about an hour's time.'

'Chess is supposed to involve a matching of intellect. You just turn it into glorified draughts.'

'Chess is a game to win if you can, and I'm trying to win right now.' Her blue eyes were wide with happiness, and her cheeks red and flushed, as she wriggled around in her chair in eagerness for my next move.

'I suppose you think you're going to swap off another of my pieces now?'

'Your move. Go on, hurry.'

'If you think you're going to do that, you've got another think coming.' I said, lowering my eyes to the board, careful not to wrinkle my head, though.

That is the way we went on – and how wrong Bunny Rexall, that shrewd man, really was as we stood together in the cloakroom, for it was impossible for me to raise the courage to make amorous advances to Margery, although Harry and each successive girl-friend spent a fair amount of their time kissing and hugging, and this was undoubtedly the proper thing to do. Margery was triangular in shape, I suppose, but she also had a face like a saint, and I was much aware of this. She was sweet, demure, serene, and would have been quite a drip had it not been for a certain vibration of her temperament that saved her from insipidity in a rather spectacular fashion : sometimes, when she was excited, I half-expected her to hum like a high-tension wire. I did kiss her once, however, not long before Mrs Ranier arrived at our place, when we were up the river with Harry and some girl, perhaps it was Clemency Bryant. We were walking by ourselves along the river bank, and in the hot stillness of the bush

we must both have felt quite different, for I was able
to put my arm around her shoulder as we went on
together, not saying much as we scuffed our feet into
the grass. Then Harry shouted for us and even as I
shouted back I recognised disappointment in her eyes,
and was made reckless, and able to give her a dab
with my lips on her cheek. She dropped her head
against my chest, turning it there so that her cheek
burned against my chest, while my voice echoed in the
river valley, like a cheer. But that was all there was
to it, and nothing happened again until after Mrs
Ranier arrived.

2

I had been stretched out on the sofa and was still in the daze induced by allowing my mind to float about in undirected thought when I stumbled out into the hallway to answer this telephone call.

'May I speak to Mrs Henderson, please?' It was a woman's voice.

'Eh?'

'Mrs Henderson, please?'

'I'm sorry – I thought you were a friend of mine – that's why I was surprised like that.'

But she ignored my apology, and announced herself as Mrs Ranier, who had arranged by mail with Mrs Henderson for accommodation, and who was now at the railway station, about to take a taxi to our place.

I told her that I would help her with her luggage when she arrived.

'Thank you so much, but the driver will do that,' she said. 'The bags are much too heavy for a boy.'

That served me right for being the little Lord Fauntleroy.

Five bedrooms, and only two of them occupied: I suppose any sensible woman like my step-mother would have rented a couple of them as soon as my father had to go to hospital, and it was obvious that money was going to be a problem. She managed very well, considering that there was nobody left of my father's family (his only brother was killed in the first world war) to help or advise her. The house was half-hearted baroque in heart timber from native forests, with fretwork pretensions dripping like lace from beneath the edges of an iron roof that was shaped and rounded in not a bad attempt at elegance. It had ceilings high enough for a manor house, and a verandah in front of the main door that had all the massiveness and solidity of a drawbridge. For some peculiar reason the house was sideways to the road, and one approached the main entrance by going through the front gate and part of the way down the side of the house by a brick path that was interrupted by another gate, this one through a trellis shield of climbing roses. This trellis gate jammed often, and had to be kicked or shouldered open: a stranger, of course, would take no such measures, and retire to the footpath to look for another entrance. There actually was one further along, but this gate was a mere hinged portion of the front tin fence, having no archway rearing up as did the other; it opened, very unobtrusively, to a path that led to the back of the house. Only an observant stranger could notice this second gate, so I dare say the less observant never did make contact with us. Inside the house, the large rooms were distributed along two passageways that were joined in a lop-sided T-shape to the line of the street. When my father died, there were two permanent bed-and-breakfast boarders with us. It was my job to take breakfast trays to them: there was old Mr Robbins, with an Oxford accent, and always smelling of drink in the morning, who delighted in telling me that he was the black sheep of the family who had outlived them all, even though he had only one kidney left; and there was Miss Rookes, a skinny old dear who peeped out from under her bedclothes and twittered, and liked me to snap up her blinds in the morning and say, 'Another new and wonderful day is here'.

A pity, that my step-mother didn't stick to such old fogies in increasing our establishment to three, although Mrs Ranier did sound like one over the telephone – an old English fogey, as I described her to Harry when he arrived a few minutes later, after crashing through the trellis gate, showering himself with rose petals, thumping across the verandah and climbing through the lounge window, pausing on the sill, his balancing knees between his hands, to give his imitation of a clucky hen. Harry's imitations were good, but simple: a lost lamb, an angry bull and a yapping dog did not require exceptional mimicry to achieve praise. When we had consumed a half-bottle of sherry at the tennis club dance not so long before he had managed a hyena laugh in the flush of the idea that he might be drunk; this was his only success outside the normal range of livestock.

Now he was jumping to the floor, hands smoothing his hair back with a quick tilting motion of his head. A couple of rose petals drifted to the floor. 'Dandruff,' he said.

I told him to shut up, that a new guest to the Hacienda Henderson (one of Harry's, that) was about to arrive and that she sounded to me like a woman with a stiff face and not much in the way of mammary glands. Then I ambled to the kitchen where my step-mother was peeling potatoes, and gave her the hurry-along: it was so typical of her that she was not prepared for Mrs Ranier, and had not even mentioned to me that she was taking on a third guest.

She beamed at my complaint, dried her hands on a tea-towel, not caring less, and saying, 'Don't fuss, it'll all be the same tomorrow'. That's how wrong she was.

On my way back to Harry, I went to the bathroom, bathed my face with a warm flannel to give tone to my skin and also did my hair with a wet comb, pushing it low and flat across my forehead in the manner of English intellectuals, at the same time allowing my jaw to hang loose while rolling my eyes to suggest twinges of decadent inspiration. This was something to try out on Harry sometime.

Harry was picking notes out on the piano in the lounge, a large square room with a green carpet about the colour of a lawn in the middle of summer, and with no more depth. The huge fireplace, the elongated sofa, the easy chairs broad enough for the rump of an elephant made it rather like the lounge of some sort of club, I suppose, but it was comfortable. My father used to play the piano; I don't know why I was never taught.

There was a scrunch of gravel on the street. Harry was immediately interested and when a car door slammed he bounced to his feet.

'I bet that's your Lady Kick-in-the-Pants,' he said. 'She'll be tootling down the path in a second.'

He crossed the room and peered out the window looking across the verandah and up the path. 'Let's prepare to survey the old tart,' he whispered, reaching up and lowering the blind to within an inch of the sill. He got to his knees and squinted underneath the blind. 'Can see every damn thing,' he said. 'Here's your mother.' Footsteps sounded across the verandah. 'She's wiping her hands on her apron, and she's heading up the path. Any minute now.'

His shoulders hunched up and wriggled about his ears. 'Strike a light,' he hissed. Now the shoulders climbed past his ears, so that only the top of his black head was visible, then fell back to reveal a twisted glimpse of his half-turned face and open mouth. 'Get over here, quick,' he said. 'Have a bloody look, man.'

I dived to my knees and scrambled across to the window.

Whether my body twitched as much as Harry's was doubtful, but my shock must have been at least as great. With my step-mother was a woman who was not so much a sight to the eyes as a punch between them; only after some blinking could a definite impression be gained of this woman. First it was her hair, shining red and smooth against her head, swelling out in a billowing wave at her shoulders; then it was her high-heeled walk, tightening and loosening the line of her skirt while her shoulders sat firmly back from the full brim of a white blouse; then it was the way her head poised in flowing balance to her motion, as though she was moving down the middle aisle of Westminster Abbey to be crowned. As she drew nearer, though, I could see that she was no beauty: her chin was sharp, her cheeks ridged and her nose pointed, and her skin was fragmented by small lines about wide eyes and wide mouth.

'She looks like a blasted witch,' Harry muttered.

'Get out of it,' I said as they reached the verandah, and pulled back from the window, dragging Harry with me in a bump to the floor.

'Holy smoke,' he gasped. 'That's a funny face, but did you see the rest of her.'

The rap of high heels on the verandah above the heavy weight of my step-mother's feet excited him and he raised and lowered himself from his sitting position by quick pushes on stiffened arms, at the same time panting loudly through an open mouth. Then he jumped to his feet and crooned, 'Not much in the way of mammary glands – that's what the boy said.'

I stood up and grabbed him by one arm, twisted him around and, moving backwards on frantic feet, pulled him to the end of the room. There, at the gap between the end of the sofa and the wall, I dropped back to the floor and with a couple of kicks of my legs roughed over the carpet on the seat of my pants, and propped my back against the wall, exclaiming in a hoarse undertone, 'Follow me.' Harry startled into almost as great an urgency, threw himself into the remaining space, severely bumping my chest. We settled down with a single grunt, with only our feet showing from behind the end of the sofa.

I listened and waited and, hearing nothing, knew that my step-mother and the woman who must be Mrs Ranier had turned down the passage. We were safe, but I had lost a considerable amount of face; to restore order to the confusion of my mind, I blew out my stomach by inflating it with as much air as could be pushed down from my lungs, held my breath for a second, and then slowly let it dribble out of my nose.

'What the heck are we doing hiding down here for?' asked Harry.

I tried to blow on my fingers as a preparation for rubbing them carefully over the knee of my right leg in a contemplative gesture, but my body was practically empty of breath and the effort merely resulted in my having to choke back air with a gasp.

'You were behaving like a madman,' I said. 'Dust got into my throat, that's why I choked.'

Then the returning vision of Mrs Ranier, a little green hat perched on top of her head like a leaf about

41

to be consumed in flame, rolling large eyes and moving her lips as though she was speaking without opening her mouth, pushed me to the verge of panic once again.

'I don't blame you for going into a flap at the sight of her,' said Harry. 'After all, she'll make a difference to you, what with her using the bathroom, et cetera.'

'I suppose so.'

'If a beautiful woman, sort of, came to my place, I'd get rattled, too. She's no chicken, so that's one consolation.'

2

My step-mother said, 'You've got your long trousers on, son.'

'I thought it was Saturday – I'm a day ahead of myself,' I said.

She let her head fall back and pushed out a hand towards me, giving that short 'Aah' as more of a snort than a laugh. I had warned her not to do that in company because, as often as not, her teeth dropped. Outside the kitchen window the morning was damp with a mist that had drifted down the river valley over the town, muffling the slow stirring of another day; the voices of children already playing in Mrs Heatley's yard were like splashes in the backwash of the river.

As for the long trousers: I wore them rather than make first acquaintance with a stranger like Mrs Ranier in the school uniform: the cap with the school insignia, navy-blue shirt unbuttoned at the neck, and the socks pulled up to just below the knee were all fair enough in their way, but having to wear short pants was the limit for somebody my age. It was the penalty for taking another year at secondary school, after matriculation. Even Harry could not look well in such an outfit, for there was no disguising how slender, almost skinny, his legs were, even though his broad shoulders and lean hips made him an otherwise impressive figure. My own legs were substantial, but the difficulty was that I had not been able to achieve a proper fit in the pants for over a year now. I had suffered from what my classmates had described as 'duck's bottom' created by a surplus material about my rump, and alterations to remedy this had resulted in an uncomfortable tightness about the crotch. Then I had discarded all the old pants, but each of the new pairs had a couple of loose inches about the waist that invariably bunched up on one side and made my hip look slightly deformed. The pair I would have to wear this day were missing the two top fly-buttons which had come off while I was practising kicking the previous day; it would probably be necessary to tighten my belt an extra notch to make sure there was no gap.

'Ready, son,' my step-mother said. 'Three this morning – there's the new one, Mrs Ranier's.' This was the first mention she had made of Mrs Ranier since her arrival; her casualness was often a blessing like that.

It was Miss Rookes' tray first. She was sitting up in bed already, a fluffy wool cardigan done up to her thin throat : she was always very careful to hide what she had nothing of.

'I see we have a new one in the back room,' she said, as I put the tray down carefully on her lap. 'I saw her as your mother was showing her about the house last night. Is she here for long?'

'I don't know,' I said, and nodded to the window,

where the blinds had been raised to flat light. The room was at the top of the main passage, and the window looked on the verandah from another angle to the main window of the lounge. 'I see the new and wonderful day has arrived already.'

'I shouldn't be surprised if she were quite happy to become a permanent in such a large room,' she said, unfolding the napkin with her little red-nailed fingers that looked like match-sticks. 'I was hoping I would get that room if it was ever opened up.'

'They look all the same to me,' I said, unable to prevent my eyes from flicking over her room, which, even if it did have the same basic furniture, was definitely made different – and cluttered – by a treadle sewing machine which she had never used, a large carved oak chest with massive silver hinges and locks, a standard lamp that required a strong band of iron to rear about six feet in ascending curves to support a tasselled red shade with a circumference of an umbrella, a large oil painting of a little girl in a hoop-skirt posing with a poodle in a garden that seemed to consist entirely of heavy dark green leaves, and a grandfather clock that was set going only occasionally, to maintain its mechanism in working order. Not visible, but most definitely in the room, too, was the dinner gong she kept just under her bed, where she could reach it by hanging over the side. It was a thing of heavy brass that swung on chains. She slept with the hammer under the pillow, and, as she had informed my step-mother on the day she arrived, the whole household should know that in the event of the gong sounding in the night it meant that there was a burglar in her room. She had a very light voice, she said, and did not trust it to carry her screams. My step-mother

44

had already been surprised by the sight of the carrier's lorry outside loaded with the new guest's possessions.

'The rooms,' Miss Rookes was saying now, 'are not quite the same – some are bigger than others.'

'They are a bit, I suppose,' I said. As I closed the door she had been about to speak again, and was lifting one hand up in an attempt to detain me, her face bright with ill-temper. It would be a pity if she stayed in this mood, because she was a nice old girl.

Mr Robbins' room was a cavern of sleep-laden darkness, and in the few seconds it took to accustom my eyes to it, I decided not to disturb the snoring mound in the bed, knowing from experience that to wake him when he was snoring was asking for trouble. It was dangerous even to pull back the drapes which were across his window and allow light to fall on eyes hooded by red-veined lids. The lids would quiver and then slide back, exposing first the deeper red of under-lids, then his bulging blue eyes would glare from the rumpled yellow flesh of his face, his gums would flop together with dry smacks, and a growling roar would begin from deep inside him, like the tired bark of an old dog. So I put the tray gently on the dressing table, brushing aside a pair of underpants that were tossed there, and tiptoed out. If Mr Robbins saw me later in the day, he would probably say, 'Thanks for the cold tea, Robert,' and his smile would briefly touch away the ageing sadness of face. At a Supreme Court session the sixth form had attended last year, a judge the spitting image of Mr Robbins was on the bench.

It was on my way back from the kitchen with Mrs Ranier's tray I first became a big joke. My sudden shiver actually jiggled the cup against the china tea-pot, as my eyes filled with the image of the woman coming down the path the previous evening, her red hair cascading down the side of her head, and falling so firmly about her shoulders that it almost seemed to be taking fresh root there, while her eyes and lips were so strangely alive, as, indeed, was her whole body. My ears even sounded with the high-heeled click of her strutting walk. In panic, I dropped on one knee outside her door and put the tray on the floor – I would knock and walk away, and she would think this procedure was the custom of the house. But then sooner or later I would be found out, and be regarded as a mere child. I had to go in. So I grabbed the doorknob, turned and pushed it in rough haste with one hand, balancing the tray with the other as I got to my feet. The door swung open and I almost leapt into the room, moving forward in a single bounding stride off my back foot. To keep balanced, I had to double over and, in taking a second stride, my knee banged the bottom of the tray. Hot tea splattered over one hand, the cup and saucer went into the air together, and the sharp bark of my breath could not be suppressed. The cup and saucer rattled back unbroken, I pivoted on my heel and brought my other hand to the tray, which then tilted, and this time the cup rolled right off the tray and bounced on the carpet, more tea spat from the spout of the pot, and the egg-cup tipped over, rolling its egg to the edge of the tray. I looked towards what I expected to be the startled figure of this new woman staring at me in fear and anger. To my left, the bottom of the bed was like the foothill of a distant mountain range whose heights disappeared into a dusk: the white covers held their pale shape as they ascended, and then the outline blurred into a formless mass. She was still asleep. I bent on one knee, dropped a groping hand to the floor and picked up the cup, keeping the tray carefully cradled with my other arm. Now I resumed my journey, keeping well over towards the foot of the bed to avoid the easy chair against the wall, and then moving around and up the side of the bed, to the little table there, all the while keeping my eyes fixed on the tray, the cup and saucer, the teapot, the toast, and the boiled egg, now out of its cup. Once the tray was awkwardly placed beside the lamp on the table, I replaced the egg and stood back and coughed.

'There's your breakfast,' I said, looking again to the bed, half-afraid that large, green, cat-like eyes would be staring at me in disapproval, and a cultured English voice would say something that would make me feel like a waiter.

But the bed was humped and silent. An outflung arm touched its edge, the palm upward, with fingers curled. A faint band of light from a gap in the window drapes illuminated the curve of the elbow where the arm was lost in the bedclothes. The darker area on the pillow was her face, the streaming smudge of grey her hair.

I turned, in the grip of a determined idea, and went across to the window. 'Your breakfast,' I said loudly, taking a drape in each hand and swishing them apart with swinging arms. The ice had to be broken somehow. The light tumbled into the room as I looked across the hedge at the wall of the house next door, trying to compose myself. 'Another new and wonderful day,' I said, thinking this might help, and looked and saw that she was lying in a twisted position, partly on her back and turned sideways below the waist, as though in the act of turning over. But she

47

was still, and seemed at first nothing much more substantial than a vivid splash of hair above the outlines of her eyes and mouth. The pallor of her tired skin matched the white of the pillow to the base of her neck, where it became tinged with yellow, only to change again to a deeper white. Then I saw the sharp rise of these two parts of her bosom as they rose under an inadequate layer of lace, like damn great mountains with wisps of cloud about their peaks. They were an awful sight, my eyes closed with a shiver of my head that drummed against my ears, and I made my way back across the room, blindly pushing my arms out ahead. You can get into hot water by breaking the ice.

The voice said, 'Hello there,' and at that same moment my leg cracked the edge of the easy chair, hurting my knee, and my eyes flew open, and the voice said, 'What's the great hurry?' It was full of warm breath, yet carried a distinct sharpness of tone. She had drawn her arms above her head and was stretching; her eyes were uncertain and still dim with sleep.

'I've brought your breakfast. It's on the table there.'

Her arms relaxed and she pulled her legs up in the bed, shut her eyes tightly, then opened them again, and it seemed incredible that they had been closed in sleep only a few seconds before, so clearly did they regard me now.

'You're the boy who answered the telephone when I rang yesterday,' she said, and I recognised the patronising tone of a grown-up being pleasant to a child.

'That's right. I am he. Robert Henderson, that is.' I tried to run my voice along the top of my mouth and clip it with my tongue against my top teeth as it

48

came out, to give it my British army officer tone, but she wriggled as she sat up and my eyes, independent of my will, lowered at the movement of her body and a noticeable lisp mixed with my words, making me sound more like a Japanese houseboy. I turned back to the door. 'Cheerio.' I mumbled that.

'Stay awhile – please.' Her voice was friendly.

'What for?'

'Well, now.' A smile flattened the points of her nose and chin. 'Is it customary for you to be so suspicious of a woman's overtures?'

There was nothing to say to her, even though I knew I must fill my gaping mouth with words, or go on looking like a stranded fish.

Her smile changed to a laugh, and she said, 'I thought you would be just the one to tell me about Albertville.'

'Are you English?'

'Goodness, yes; also a lot of other things I suppose.' She was surprised, and not unfriendly, and this made me feel a little better.

'Your accent . . . it's English, that's why I ask.'

'You funny boy. I used to be an amateur actress of sorts, so perhaps I've got what is best described as a repertory accent.'

'I'm seventeen, and not exactly a boy. I suppose anyone your age might think that's not very old, though.'

Mrs Ranier flopped back to the pillow and pulled the bed-cover over her head and, though I was not certain, she seemed to be giggling. When she revealed herself again, she was solemn and witch-like through the tangled mass of her hair; there was no doubt that her face was quite sharp in repose. She was not really

49

unattractive, but there was a vague twist, a slight grimace of her features that was not exactly pleasant; her nose and chin, for instance, were slightly out of whack. And only her cheeks seemed completely free of the delicate lines that traced about her face, here and there actually becoming wrinkles. Her wide mouth and large eyes saved her: they seemed so ready for laughter that it was impossible to think her ugly. She was unusual, that was all, and certain to look a little better with her make-up on, too. And her eyes were kind.

Her eyes: 'I'll be darned,' I said. 'Your eyes are not green, they're blue.'

'Well, then, I'll be darned, too. My eyes are blue, you're not a boy. I'm English, and, darn me again, I'm not really very old – I'm only thirty-one.'

'It's just that I thought your eyes were green, that's all.'

'Don't apologise,' she said, shaking her head, and then pushing her hair back from her face with a long white hand. 'Incidentally, you gave me quite a fright, waking up as I did and seeing a man – a man, I said – running across my bedroom.'

'I was hurrying because I have a lot to do today.'

'I won't keep you.' She pulled her knees up and leaned forward and wrapped her arms about them. This was much better, as only her shoulders and arms were visible now. 'As a matter of fact, now I am able to really see you, and see what a pleasant-looking young man you are, I feel . . . lonely is the word. I haven't spoken to anybody in a friendly way for days want to know something about Albertville.'

'I've lived in Albertville all my life. I was born and

bred here, and – that's extremely decent of you Mrs Ranier, to want to talk to me. Except that I've got to go pretty soon.'

'Friends, then? I thought for a moment, the way you were glaring at me, that we were going to be enemies.' She was so friendly, and regarding me more as an equal, that I was able to say, 'I suppose I was a little childlike, going on the way I did.' I actually did smile at her, too.

'Gracious me, that's a handsome smile,' she said.

Of course I blushed.

'It really is,' she said, turning and leaning over the tray to pour herself a cup of tea. 'What's the local transport? That's one of the things I'd like to know about.'

'Trams,' I said, amazed that the distress did not sound in my voice. My eyes jumped up to stare at the picture of the barges on the River Thames above her bed, away from the inflated tightness of her body that was overflowing the lace frill of the silk nightgown, as the thin shoulder-strap buried into flesh at the stretch of her reaching arm.

'Trams every half-hour or so in the main streets, and buses for any distance,' I said, concentrating on the barges: there were five of them in a wet line, in ghostly movement through the white wisps of mist, and far behind and high above them, touched by the rising sun, the towers of the Houses of Parliament glistened.

'And about meals – where would be the best place for me to eat?'

I was looking away from the Thames barges now, out the windows again, where the drapes allowed the well-washed lace of the curtains to frame a view of the heavy bush of rhododendrons backing against the green hedge, beyond which was the blank wall of the neighbouring house.

'There's the hotels, for good meals, and there's a couple of restaurants in town, too.'

She laughed again. 'Really, I'm sorry to be so boring, but I have to know these things. What on earth are you looking at?'

Desperately: the brown-leaf wallpaper, the picture rail, the dark ceiling; then back to those Thames barges. 'I've never really looked at that picture before,' I said. 'It took my fancy, that's all.'

There was a scrape of a cup on a saucer. I looked down and saw that she was again hunched over her knees, on which she was now balancing her tea. She was quite decent again, but my ears had begun to throb and wriggling black lines floated lazily across my vision, and my stomach lurched. The strain was beginning to tell.

'Cheerio,' I said, turning towards the door.

'Wait, please – a couple more questions first,' she said.

I had skipped my feet and was saying, 'Later,' when the door bumped against my shoulders. I glanced back at her and bared my teeth into as big a smile as possible and said, 'I'll see you later – I'm in a hurry.' She was staring after me, cup nearly to her lips, and there was the oddest expression on her odd face.

Back in the kitchen for my own breakfast, and my step-mother was asking me, 'How's everybody this morning, son?'

I looked carefully out the window: the dullness of the air was clearing and the first shine of sun was there.

'They are all right,' I said, and was surprised that I could sound so absent-minded.

Mrs Blake was standing at the back door. She was looking out across the backyard with what I judged to be a pleased look, though her countenance was not a reliable guide to any of her moods. She was a very thin woman who treated her feelings as private, and was greatly helped in their disguise by eyes that had a dislocated focus which made it impossible to study her closely without being sure that she was returning your gaze. But there was no doubt now that she was staring over the hedge that separated the concrete area about the foot of the steps from the rest of the backyard – staring with a concentration that almost righted her eyes as she watched Mr Blake digging.

'Gardening, eh?' I said.

She gave the laugh that Harry admired so much; it sounded like the low clucking of a worried hen. 'Yes, and he's started about a month too late,' she said. 'I've been telling him about it for ages, and now he's started like a demon, when the ground is not any too easy.'

Mr Blake, who was chief clerk of the Metropolitan Life Insurance office, was a powerful man, with great chunks of weight about his hips and shoulders, arms as thick as my legs, and hands the size of soup plates. Until I met him I had not realised there were such things as face muscles: his were plaited in thick strands about his cheekbones and chin, and bunched when he set his jaws. In his youth he had been a good front-row forward and had represented the North Island for two years. Margery had shown me his book of press clippings and it was noticeable how often he was described as ferocious. He was intelligent, but nevertheless it was astounding that he should earn his living by juggling mere figures. Now he was digging the ragged ground of his garden with a pumping motion of the spade, down, up, over, throwing large clumps of shattering earth in a sweat of movement like a crazed pirate after treasure. Already the weeds and rank grass, mixed with the wild growth of sprouts from a previous potato crop, and the brown wisps of last season's beans, were uprooted and scattered under the flying earth.

'There'll be plenty of time,' I said. 'Where's Margery, Mrs Blake?' I had been wrong about her mood again; she was certainly not pleased.

Mrs Blake stepped down from the doorway. 'Go on in, Robert. She's probably in the lounge.' Her gaze was still concentrated on her husband, waiting for him to slacken his efforts, so that he would have to listen to what she wanted to say. She was the nagging type.

'Anybody home?'

'Down here.' Margery's voice floated down from the front of the house without interest or enthusiasm. I went from the kitchen through the living room (with its spindle-legged furniture I didn't like), looking forward to her. I was not afraid of Margery, and she was nearly a woman; I would be able to talk to her about Mrs Ranier.

She was in the lounge sprawled on the sofa, one leg dropping to the floor, and I noticed for the first time that she was like her father. It was her position, which emphasized the width of her hips, that pointed up the resemblance.

'Oh, hello,' she said.

'What ails thee?'

'Nothing. I'm bored, that's all, and even playing the

piano hasn't helped. Mother and father are at logger-
heads, we're not doing anything interesting tonight.
What a life. It's very bad when music doesn't help.'

The baby grand piano gleamed darkly from the
front corner of the room, where it stood in what I
regarded as a truly classic position: behind were the
bay windows, grand enough to be looking out on some
terraced garden sprinkled with odd pieces of statuary
about which strutted moonlight peacocks in scented
air. On top of the piano were sheaves of sheet music
that could have been disturbed by passionate hands,
à la Chopin, or any of that push. It seemed incredible
that Margery could be bored.

'Well, cheer up, old thing,' I said. 'Let joy be unconfined, because Robert the wonderful is here.'

'Don't be asinine.'

'Eh?'

'Don't you think you should avoid trying to sound
like Harry? The bouncing good-humour rôle doesn't
suit you at all. It is simply not appropriate to your
character.'

I stared at the carelessness of her sloppy blue
sweater far down over the top of the crumpled pleats
of her grey skirt, and at the disjointed hang of her
leg to the floor, the hunch-shouldered, stiff-necked,
flop-armed sprawl of her body, and spluttered, 'Well,
I like that.' For effect, I paused and pointedly moved
my eyes the awkward journey from her head to toe.
'And do you think you are appropriate, flopping
around like that? Who do you think you are? Camille
or somebody?'

She squeaked softly and sat up in a fluster of arms
and legs. 'At least I don't imitate immature friends,'
she said in a high voice. 'What have you come

55

around here for anyway? I don't remember asking you.'

'It's Friday, isn't it? I always come around on Fridays, even if we aren't doing anything. Not that I haven't anything better to do, don't you worry. What's all this immaturity business? What are you hinting at?'

'I told you. "Let joy be unconfined, because Robert the wonderful is here." That's something Harry would say.'

I gestured towards her with my foot. 'What have you got against Harry all of a sudden? What are you picking on him for?'

'You're not Harry, that's all.'

'Ha-ha,' I said, seeing my chance. 'That's a load off my mind. I've been wondering for days now, and once or twice at night. Am I Harry, I've asked myself. I don't know, I've answered. Find out, I've told myself. And now you've come to my rescue. I'm not Harry, you tell me.' I spread my arms out, confident that I had achieved a clear edge on her, and backed across the room to where there was a chair. As soon as I felt it against my legs, I allowed myself to fall backwards, with a loud huff of breath. 'Oh! the relief,' I cried. 'How can I ever thank you?' Even though the arm of the chair had jabbed me hard on one side of my back – my fall had been timed carelessly – and I had to roll to one side to finally get into position, my act was pretty good.

'That's Daddy's chair, and you know the rule that nobody else is allowed to use it,' Margery said. She perched on the edge of the sofa, as though she were trying to draw herself to her full height without standing. 'Get out of it this minute. You ought to be ashamed of yourself smashing into it like that. Get out, this minute.'

I straightened in the chair. 'Your hair is sticking out all over the place, you look like nothing on earth, you insult me, you insult my best friend, and now you're ordering me out. I'll show you, Margery – I'll jolly well go, if you're not careful.'

She ran her hands back under her hair and pressed her head as though she was in pain, and the flush on her cheeks spread and deepened, and her mouth dropped at the corners as ripples of tightening muscles pulled down from her neck. I felt my own anger die in the face of her fury like a spluttering match against a bonfire.

'How dare you talk to me like that, Robert Henderson. You rude, unmannerly wretch – leave this house this minute.'

I leapt from the chair and strode across the room, at the same time giving quite a good snap of my fingers. 'I had made up my mind to go as soon as I looked into this room,' I said. 'I was just hanging around to break it to you gently.' I lowered my voice to a dignified bass, acquitting myself very well. 'Pardon my intrusion, you bad-tempered, ill-bred female.' It had to be made obvious to her that she had insulted an adult.

Mrs Blake, still standing at the bottom of the back steps, seemed to look at me as I left. She said, 'Going so soon, Robert?'

'Just dropped in for a minute, Mrs Blake,' I said, with dignity.

Mr Blake was still digging with the same intensity, but now his breathing had become so heavy and his bulk and movement so blurred in the dusk that he looked like some wild animal scavenging for food. A pig, perhaps.

'He won't stop,' said Mrs Blake. 'He knows I'm watching and he won't look up or stop.'

I went through Massey Street to the top of Victoria Avenue and walked down as far as the corner of Hobson Street before turning off to the top of the slight rise above there; one more turn took me into Wakefield Street, and home. All the way I was a mixture of panic and temper: the intermittent glow of the avenue lights and the narrow strip of constant illumination that was the bridge across the Albert invited me to break into a gallop, all the way to the bridge, to cross over it, and keep on galloping, never to come back. Then I wanted to turn back and storm in on Margery's place and tell her what a stupid, a really stupid, person she had the misfortune to be. I hesitated at the corner of Albert Street, wondering whether I should go on down to Tony's milk-bar for a drink. Harry was probably down there with one of his girls; these days he was content to spend an hour with them at a milk-bar, in preference to the pictures, because it gave him more wooing time, he said. But I decided that the sight of him making so much progress towards sexual maturity would be depressing, and kept on heading for home. It occurred to me that being kissed only once in the past eight months was a possible reason for Margery's vile temper. I felt greatly handicapped by living in a place like New Zealand: anywhere else, such as Europe or America, a chap could save up his pocket money and go to one of those houses of ill-fame and make up a lot of lost ground; he wouldn't, of course, do anything degrading with those girls, and they'd appreciate it; but he'd have a good yarn with them, practice kissing on them, and generally pick up experience.

I slammed the front gate back with unnecessary force, kicked it shut with a thump of my heel, walked down the brick path, pushed the trellis gate open with a hard slap of my hands, and stalked around the side of the house.

'Goodness, is this my young man of the breakfast tray?' a voice asked. Sure enough, it was Mrs Ranier, sitting on the verandah in a chair by the lounge window, robbed by the dusk of colour and shape; she could be any specimen of the opposite sex, which was no recommendation.

It was nearly dark, and I would not have to disguise my feelings, or worry how she looked: in another few minutes she could be naked and dancing around the verandah, without any embarrassment to me, unless her skin was luminous. It occurred to me that I should insult her in some way, to get even with her.

'You burst around there like a tornado,' she said.

'I was thinking,' I snapped.

'Then you must have been contemplating what you would like to do with your worst enemy.'

She was more than a voice. Her hair had a slight glow of colour, and little chips of light marked her eyes as she sat on the old sea-grass chair that was always left out there. The shape of the house huddled over her, giving no sign of life except for the dull glare of the hall light through the tinted glass of the upper half of the front door. I glared down at her outline, full of the courage of my irritation in the gloom.

'There are a few people I don't like,' I said.

'Oh?' She hesitated. 'I hope I'm not one of them.'

'You might be.'

She laughed. 'Young man – you don't know me well enough to dislike me.'

'I get fed up, that's all.'

'Sit down and talk about it, then. I'm sitting here brooding myself. We might do each other some good.'

She had a juicy voice; it was probably costing her some effort not to dribble. I walked over and carefully sat down on the edge of the verandah, propping one elbow on my knee and cupping my face in my hand, rather wishing it was not dark after all, as I knew that in such a pose it would be clear that I was nobody's fool.

'You're married, and well and truly grown up,' I said. 'You've no reason to brood. At my age, smacking into problems for the first time, there's more reason to.'

'Familiarity with problems doesn't make them any easier,' she said. 'Harder, perhaps, because you aren't so hopeful as when you first met them.'

'Perhaps you're right. Although familiarity with some problems must help. With people, for instance.'

'Girls, for instance?' she said.

'I suppose so.'

'I thought as much.'

'Do you mean men?' I asked, determined to keep up with her.

She laughed, and answered, 'I suppose so,' and her hand brushed past my ear and flicked up the back of my neck, tingling the roots of my hair and sending a chain reaction banging down my spine. 'I used to have a brother like you,' she said.

I could not help making a slight yipping noise as I tried to clear my throat. My spine was giving me hell.

She went on. 'I must confess that I can't really claim to know more about men now than when I was sixteen.'

60

'I'm just seventeen, Mrs Ranier,' I said.

'My brother was killed in the war. He was only nineteen.'

'I'm sorry,' I said, though this didn't mean much to me, of course.

Her chair creaked, and by squinting hard I saw that she had leaned back, and was not in a position to reach out and touch me again. Rather than have to put up with any sad silence, I said, 'Have you ever travelled?'

'I've been to France, America, places,' she said, quite attentively.

'London and New York, and places like that – you've been there?'

'Yes.'

Happier now, I rubbed my hands up and down the side of my legs and turned towards her. 'What are you doing here then?'

'Oh.' She didn't seem pleased. 'Now that is what I was brooding about a few moments ago.'

'I'm sorry,' I said. 'I didn't mean it that way – I'm quite glad you're here, myself. What I meant was – well, you know.'

'I know,' she said.

'Isn't it funny, but when you spoke to me over the telephone I knew you were an overseas type. That was the one thing I was right about – I'm not sure, but I even thought about New York, as well as London.'

'Well, I've only been in New Zealand for two years, so you're a good judge.' She added with unmistakeable feeling, 'I hated coming here.'

'You've been very lucky to travel like that, and I can see New Zealand could be a slight let-down, and there's no place like . . . the old native soil, I suppose.'

I had been about to say 'like home', but realised in time that it was a cliché. I added, 'What does Mr Ranier think?'

'He doesn't.' Again there was no mistaking her tone, and in momentary fright I asked, 'Where's Mr Ranier now?' with all the impertinence of impulse.

'You're an inquisitive young devil,' she said. 'Nothing but personal questions.'

'I'm sorry.'

'Don't be – I think I asked for it.' She must have leaned forward because her voice was much closer now. 'As a matter of fact, I'm one of those women who were married but who are not any longer – I'm divorced. A failed war bride, that's it.'

I stuttered my way out of that hole, scarcely able to think, although I was vaguely conscious of apologising again for being personal, and thinking that here was the reason for her not being embarrassed by my seeing her in bed with so little on: being divorced she had left that kind of business far behind.

'I should ask *you* some personal questions,' she said after a while.

'That's all right,' I said. 'But I've got a few secrets.'

'Try to keep it that way, old chap,' she laughed. 'Why aren't you out on a Friday night, for instance?'

'There – there's a secret.'

'Girl trouble?'

I hunched up over my knees, very pleased that the night was a wet blanket for somebody who was embarrassing me: she wouldn't be very impressed by a seventeen-year-old who turned scarlet at the very mention of girl-trouble.

'I haven't got any brothers or sisters,' I said. 'I think I miss having a sister the most.'

3

This morning she did not bother to sit up, but only stared at the ceiling with the fixity of unconsciousness. Having heard of people who slept with their eyes open, I was beginning to wonder if she was like that when she spoke. 'Thank God for Robert Henderson,' she said. 'In another moment I might have screamed.' There was no mistaking the sadness of her voice, so I tried to be cheerful.

She turned over to face me, propping herself up on her elbow, sleepy and melancholy. 'You smug young New Zealander,' she said.

'That's all right about that,' I said. 'I like being a New Zealander.'

'There are better places, believe me.'

'Is that so,' I answered, anxious to display my wares. 'Well now, you shouldn't be so hard on us. There is nothing wrong with our blood and bone and guts and stuff and our brains and our land is as good as anybody else's.'

'Goodness,' she said, starting to brighten, anything but sleep in her blue-gleaming eyes, a growing smile that blunted the tip of her nose (strange, her having there what anywhere else would be a dimple) and making a pale crinkle of her forehead under the red tangle of her hair.

'The British must be a great people and I've had a lot of their history stuffed down my throat and the Americans are a great people, too, and I've had a lot

63

of them stuffed down my throat. Yet it's funny that nobody stuffs anything down my throat about being a New Zealander.'

'You are a patriot,' she said, holding this smile.

I nodded, encouraged by the effect I was having on her. 'I want to look like a New Zealander, speak like one and think like one.'

'You darling – you haven't a hope,' she laughed. 'All the old ladies and the politicians spout love for Britain, the men go overseas and get killed and maimed for Britain, and all the best people try and speak with a correct English accent——'

'Oh, well.'

'And right now girls your own age in Wellington are aching to make their début at Government House in front of a Governor-General who is probably a bored old English fool who has been given the post as a reward for third-class service to the Crown.'

'Yes, but——'

'And your other teen-agers are swooning over Frank Sinatra or dreaming about Betty Grable.'

'You don't seem to like the place,' I said, a little annoyed.

'I don't like imitations, Robbie.'

'I hope I'm no darned imitation.'

'No, old chap,' she said, 'you're an original, bless you.'

'Don't start teasing me now.'

'You're slightly awkward, pure-hearted, clear-eyed, mentally and physically strong, and possess an indefinable quality that suggests you have depths of divine decency to draw upon.'

'A – ooh,' I gasped. 'You're weird and wonderful . . . you're . . . heck, I can't compete with you in describing people.'

'You're not really handsome, Mr Henderson. You're a male beauty, that's all.'

I closed my eyes as I rubbed a hand across my prickling forehead. 'Stop teasing me, Mrs Ranier,' I said. 'Honestly, I can't really get to the bottom of this teasing. It's awfully embarrassing, y'know. Please stop.'

'O.K. kid and righty ho old top.'

2

She took a part-time job in a bookshop in Maria Place, working five hours a day, most of the time in sole charge: there was hardly enough room for her and the proprietor both to be in there at one time. This bookshop was not much bigger than a cupboard, with a plate-glass window instead of a door to the pavement outside. Looking in at her from the street to where she sat behind the counter, surrounded by shelves of books, racks of magazines and periodicals, with copies of the *Dominion*, from Wellington, and our own local paper, the *Herald*, in separate piles at each end of the counter, I thought that she was really a creature that belonged to an existence of words alone: words about the big cities and exotic places and people much larger than the life around me: only books conveyed permanent knowledge of such life to Albertville. The films brought them too, but films moved on and were forgotten: the printed word remained.

This morning, cradling the tray with one arm, I knocked on her door once, hard, thrust it open and stepped into the room, not allowing myself time for second thoughts. Hers was the largest room in the house, as Miss Rookes hinted. The double-bed was still there: Mrs Ranier had already bounced up and down in it and proclaimed that it was a double-bed with a single-bed mind. I very nearly saw the joke, and smiled. There was a wardrobe in the room about eight feet high, with enough width to make it seem squat: the oval mirror on the door was big enough to reflect a whole family. Everything was big about the room: that bedside table was about the size of a kitchen table, the dressing table had umpteen drawers, and another mirror which, although it wasn't as big, could at least stare back at the wardrobe mirror. A couple of easy chairs with faded covers left over from the old lounge suite filled a couple of gaps, and another table, shining black, filled a corner next to the window. The hulking double-bed was not exactly out of place: it had a white cover, incidentally, which looked like a giant damask table napkin. But the carpet, of course, couldn't cope with all this size, and made a square centred in the middle of the room, the edges of which fell a good four feet short of the walls; the intervening bare space had been stained, and kept a reasonable polish.

This morning, however, my first sight when I opened the door was of the open window way across the room, with a wind stirring the parted velvet drapes.

'Is that you?' her voice said, and even as I looked I thought she sounded different. She was different, too. She was upside-down on the bed.

'Crikey,' I said. The cup slid from one end of the tray to the other, sideswiping the teapot on the way.

Her head and shoulders were on the bed, but her legs, encased in flapping silk, were waving in the air, while her body was propped on bent arms, with balancing hands pressed firmly against her back. Her toe-nails were red, her feet small, her legs, revealed to the knees by the loose fall of the silk, were the colour of cream, but the twist of her body and her movements made it difficult for me to assess exactly what else there was of this woman before I hastily returned my eyes to the unstable tray.

'For the waist-line,' she said breathlessly. 'I've just got the rhythm, I think.'

I looked back to her, at the confusion of red hair on the white bedcover, the inverted bright eyes, the cheeks as pink as her lips, the point of her chin hard against the base of her neck, marking the exact centre of a crease of flesh that ran in a circle from ear to ear. She was at least decent, I thought at first, noting the bunch of her pyjama top against her chin. And then I saw that this bunching had been gained only at the price of exposing her midriff, and that the flailing motion of her legs was slowly increasing the exposure until she was no more decent than she usually was, except that this time the view was from a different direction.

I could only move slowly, as though great weights were fixed to my feet, around the foot of the bed, towards the bedside table, and by the time I had actually put the tray down, it seemed that minutes had passed since I had started on the journey; minutes full of the sound of little puffs of her breath.

I took a step back from the table, desperate with anxiety, the bedsprings creaked with the fall of her body, drawing my eyes around to the sight of her sprawling on her stomach across the bed.

'Phew,' she said loudly, and it was as though she had just flung herself to the ground after a headlong

67

chase, so hot were her cheeks and eyes, and dishevelled was her hair. She smiled at me. 'For some reason I felt energetic this morning.'

'Yes,' I said.

'Some ass was singing in the bathroom and woke me up, and I felt absolutely full of exercise.'

'Oh.' That ass was me, of course.

'And I really need a cup of tea, Robbie, you blessed boy.'

'That's good.'

She rolled over towards the top of the bed, pulled the bedclothes back and wriggled underneath, setting in independent motion the upper part of her body.

'I've been thinking about your attitude to women, old man.'

'Oh?' I said, even more afraid. This would be about the fourth time she'd pulled my leg about girls.

'Yes. I've decided that you are a handsome young man, and that you are unaware of the fact. This is a virtue up to a point, but I feel it is time you should exert your charm more aggressively.' She beamed. 'You're too shy, bless you; I feel positive you've never kissed a girl.'

The feeling of hollow weakness and embarrassment left me and I was saying loudly, 'That's not right, Mrs Ranier,' and I was actually staring right at her, clenching my hands, not caring what I saw, but caring very much what she had said. 'I have so,' I said into her smile. 'And I am not shy.'

Now she laughed. 'Oh, you are angry at me.' She held out her hand and said, 'Come here, if you're not shy.' I moved the step across to the side of the bed. She took my hand. 'Sit down, silly,' she said, and I sat down, and she was smiling into my face. 'How often?'

she said. Her breath was as warm as her hair looked, and her hand was hot. I hated the sight and feel of her.

'It's not your business.'

'Show me,' she said. 'Go on, if you are not shy.'

It was almost as though I had lost my temper; I hated her, and felt like hitting her, and would rather die than let her humiliate me; my eyes closed and I jabbed my mouth at her face.

'There,' I said, pulling my face back and opening my eyes. Her eyes were just opening, too.

'On the forehead, just as I thought,' she said, and her hands were up to my shoulders now, pulling me forward. 'You should do it like this.' And there was wet heat against my mouth, wet, and then she was laughing away from me, and pushing me back.

'That's much the better way to kiss a girl,' she said.

'Oh,' I said, and stood up, not actually seeing her any longer. 'Thank you.' I said that, too, and was certain I was not seeing anything: she had disappeared: the bed, the room, perhaps even the whole house, had all gone, and I was alone in an invisible somewhere. But then I had heard myself speak, and there was solidity under my moving feet.

'Don't look quite so offended, Robert; I was only teasing you.'

That was her speaking; I could hear her quite clearly. And now there was a light in my eyes, shattering into fragments of colour that took form and substance, and I was staring across at her, even as I was actually backing around the bed towards the door.

'That's all right,' I said.

'But why are you leaving?'

'It's just that I'm in a hurry, this morning.'

She shook her head, laughing. 'Goodbye, then.'
'Cheerio, Mrs Ranier.'

3

Telling Harry about her – at least trying to tell him: this would be one of the times that I hated her, and a Saturday afternoon, because we were drifting down to Tony's milk-bar. Something had happened during the night, and she was the subject of my dream. I had told myself that it was not my fault: Mr Pringle, the athletics master, had given the senior boys an impromptu little lecture on the subject not so long before, and had stressed the fact that it was a perfectly normal and healthy occurrence, as long as it was not self-induced.

This afternoon was a straggler left behind by winter, the wind was clipping our ears, the sky was a mess of dung clouds, I couldn't hold out on Harry any longer, although I toughened it all up a little, of course, and told him that Mrs Ranier was a bloody nuisance.

'I'm all ears,' he said, jostling his shoulder against mine.

'She shows too much,' I said. 'It's more than that, I think. But that's what I can be definite about, her showing too much.'

'By heck! What do you mean?' He was almost pushing me off the footpath now.

'In the morning, when I take her the breakfast tray. She wears these things about her . . . her chest. They might be nightgowns, or pyjamas, even. Whatever they happen to be, they aren't much.'

'You mean she shows her bangers?'

70

'What she shows is nobody's business. At least it shouldn't be anybody's business.'

'You mean you see them?'

'I just about drop dead, and all she does is engage me in conversation.'

Harry veered back towards the other side of the footpath, frowning. 'What do they look like?' he asked.

'What do you mean?'

'What do you think I mean? Her bangers, of course.' His voice was sharp, and I was going to seem a fool to his eyes by showing my upset.

'She has a very good physique,' I said. 'It doesn't matter, though. It doesn't really worry me. It's her sarcastic tongue that annoys me, now that I think of it.'

'You blasé intellectual again,' muttered Harry.

Sure that he was feeling the first twinges of contempt for me, I pulled back into my shell when he started asking me questions. This irritated him, naturally, but I didn't mind his irritation. All the way down the avenue we bickered back and forth, without my really telling him any more, and then we sat in one of the plywood cubicles of the milk-bar, across from the shining length of the counter, where Tony's wife was leaning amid the pump handles and mix machines, listening to a jukebox record of some woman singing about how she was going to love some man in a manner to which hitherto he had not been accustomed. Everybody there, all the chaps and girls, were listening to the damn thing, while I wondered whether there was some sense in such blasted tripe, and whether the phrases were keys that unlocked whole new worlds of emotion and feeling. There had to be something to a business that attracted all age groups, because Tony's wife, no chicken, was entranced, too.

I thought of Harry, always in the top ten of the class, a really outstanding sport, who was never rattled by women, though, being a good all-rounder, he gave them plenty of his spare time. This last year, ever since getting a start with Jillian, he had gone from one girl to the other, not pausing for breath. If our positions were reversed, I supposed, Harry would sail into Mrs Ranier's bedroom without embarrassment, wake her up by loud bugling noises, and then sit on the edge of the bed and chew a piece of her toast, not giving a threepenny bit for what he saw, or how she teased him.

Now he was slapping a hand behind my neck. 'Don't look so worried, Roberto,' he said, loudly. 'If this red-haired oo-la-la gets out of hand I'll fix her for you.'

4

This last football game of the season was on the next Tuesday, a few weeks after the real end of the season because the other school, Palmerston North, had had an epidemic of measles. The team and three bus-loads of their ra-ra supporters arrived about midday, and, of course, we made the obvious jokes about knocking the spots off them, but we didn't have much hope of that: a bigger school, they nearly always had the edge on us, especially in the forwards. Our ground was beyond the tennis courts, far back from the New Wing. The poplar trees that marked the school boundary were only about ten yards away on the sideline on the far side, the spire of St John's Presbyterian Church was like an extension of a goal-post at one end, and third-formers perched on the precarious grandstand that was the board fence behind the other. The slope down from the tennis courts was terraced, with sitting room for a couple of hundred spectators on the near side. One ivy wall of the Old Building could be seen at an angle from the half-way mark, so there was a touch of the old school atmosphere. The rear view of the New Wing was simply the top of bare wall-board, viewed through the wire-netting around the courts. If the third-formers perched like birds on the fence, the girls actually looked and sounded like birds, behind the posts at the steeple end : they were magpies in their black gym frocks and white blouses, with their shrilling and chattering. Most of the chaps were on the far sideline, leaving the terrace to the visitors: there was actually quite a crowd, all told, and the day was cold but fine, and in the distance plateau hills were green, and everybody seemed excited, but I could not share in it. The visiting team had the cloakroom as a dressing shed, and we used the classroom next door. Sprigs clattering on the floor, knees, jocks, backsides and shouting as everybody dressed, the long run from the New Wing around the tennis courts and down the slope to the field, the school cheers, the wait for the referee's whistle, the kick-off – and all the time I hardly felt a damned thing, because for the first time, a game really didn't seem important. But when their forwards came through with the ball at their toes I did my job and went right in on top of the ball. Boots were flying in the ruck that followed, and I was still buried under heap of casualties when one of their backs bolted in right under the posts to score.

Five minutes later they scored again. This time I was buried on the half-way line. It was bloody, really. Hutchie, our coach, screamed at our forwards from the

73

side-line, and with considerable justification, for they were behaving like a bunch of children at a lolly scramble. Apart from Hutchie's high-pitched disgust, the only other sound was the three bus-loads of cheering that Palmerston had brought with them. Brian Pinnington, our captain, smacked his fist into his hand as he spoke to the forwards. Standing at full-back I began to feel something, too, and looked up at the cold blue sky and thought that this really was important and that this bitch didn't matter. This bitch was Mrs Ranier, of course. Our chaps up front really got going now and charged into rucks like maddened young bulls and a minute later, deep into Palmerston territory, a clearing kick by their half-back came straight into my hands. My drop-kick from almost in front went straight between the posts. There was much cheering, of course, and the idea of Margery being among all those magpies didn't do me any harm. I got two more penalties, fairly easy ones, bang, bang, just like that, so we were only one point down at half-time. But within five minutes of the start of the second spell their little half-back nipped around a scrum, got clean through our defence, zigged as I zagged, and scored. The kick put us six points down. Then Harry made a good run on the wing, his legs moving in a circular blur that suggested he was riding an invisible bicycle – he had nearly scored when somebody pushed him off it. Palmerston's defence was just too good. This, the slight breeze from behind and my inflation by earlier success led to my trying a penalty from near the half-way mark. Ordinarily I would not have risked looking the complete idiot. Now I kicked and nearly fractured my jaw on my knee on the follow-through while the ball sailed over as though it had no choice.

74

From then on, it was all down-hill. They missed a couple of kicks, and shortly after I got another, and that evened the score. Then, right on full-time, their side-row man was a mile offside in a ruck, the ref's whistle went, and there it was, a penalty from near touch on the twenty-five-yard line. The chaps on the sideline had to stand back and make a channel for my run-up for this last kick, and as soon as it smacked over they were all over me, clutching, pushing, slapping and cheering. The referee blew full-time in the middle of it all, and the whole damned school seemed to be on my back. When they finally shouldered me into the air, the girls were on the fringes of the mob. It was all like coming out from under an anaesthetic and discovering you had been made a king. The team formed a wedge around the chaps who were carrying me, and ran me right across the paddock. Hutchie, who had never really thought much of my football, bounced around among the chaps, looking a lot less than the old battle-axe he really was, and clutched my leg and yelled, 'It's a record, Henderson – eighteen points is a record.'

They wouldn't let me down when we got to the terrace, but shouldered me around the crowd and up the slope. Even as I wobbled about up there, I was looking around, half-hoping that I would see Margery and be able to wave to her. Instead, I saw Mrs Ranier, standing right at the top of the terrace in a thick brown coat, the collar turned right up past her ears. She had a yellow scarf around her head, and her hands were thrust deep into the pockets of her coat. She simply stared across at me and did not smile as I was lugged and jolted up the slope. She was not far away. I felt as though her face was right up against mine. I swear I could even smell her. I twisted my head down as I was lugged and jolted up this slope and shouted, 'Harry.' He was one of the chaps shouldering me, of course, and concentrating too hard on his foothold to pay any attention, so I waited until we were at the top, going around the tennis courts, and shouted again, 'Harry.' This mob were staying with us, though, and making some hullabaloo, and when he looked up at me, with a grin wide enough to split his tired face, I could only hit my fists on the top of his head, pretending that I wanted to share this success business with him.

Inside the building and our dressing room, when the team started to get personal about the game, I forgot about Mrs Ranier. Brian Pinnington slapped his hand on my shoulder and said, 'I dub thee "Boot" Henderson,' a nickname that was to stick. The headmaster came in and tossed congratulations around, with special mention of me. It all helped, I suppose.

5

Margery was impressed when I saw her that evening. Her father was impressed, too, and we had to listen to some of his reminiscing. Whenever possible I studied Margery, and felt especially happy with her face: soon, I thought, I'll tell her she is pretty. Though she was not exactly sports-minded, she said I was wonderful. I kissed her for the second time this night.

She came to the gate with me when I left at nine o'clock, and in the dark shadow of the garage I took her by the arm and bent over her, and when she looked up, pressed my mouth firmly down on her face and held it there for a few seconds. Being desperate, I could not be sure exactly where I kissed her, but afterwards I remembered that at our first contact she shifted slightly, and I was fairly certain that this was to try and get her lips fully against mine, and that she was responding readily. I did not wait to find out exactly what she thought about it, however, because as soon as I lifted my face away from her – it was necessary to stop in order to take a breath – I released her arm and stepped right away from her, out through the gate to the footpath, and said, 'Well, goodnight.'

'Goodnight.' She sounded out of breath, too.

6

Next morning I woke up almost light-hearted in my thoughts of Mrs Ranier, and reasoned that a couple of extra slabs of flesh could be expected to send even an intelligent person like me into a dither, and that it was a pity that sex was a one-way traffic. If women got into a dither about it, I thought, it would be revenge to have Mrs Ranier bring me breakfast in bed. I could see myself, lolling back with the three top buttons of my pyjama coat unbuttoned when she brought the tray, my coat would part to reveal my tanned chest and she would grow pale, perhaps gasp slightly.

'Thank you, Mrs Ranier,' I would say, slyly observing her from under lowered eyelids.

When the alarm clock went off I was running through other such scenes with Mrs Ranier, including one in which she had walked into the bathroom and found me clad only in my underpants and singlet as

I brushed my teeth. She fell heavily against the caliphont in her agitation.

I rolled out of bed, stripped off my pyjamas and stared at my naked body in the wardrobe mirror. Not bad, I thought, although there was absolutely no sign of any hair on my chest, and my biceps were not really thick enough. It was also a little disappointing that I did not have to shave regularly, while Harry was getting a growth that required attention every other day; Harry was also circumcized, and I was not, but I could not feel that I was at any real disadvantage there, unless something was involved that I did not know about yet, which was not unlikely.

In my underclothes I went to the window and did deep-breathing exercises with rising optimism. 'Fresh morning gusts have blown away all fear from my glad bosom,' I recited aloud, and immediately wished I could remember how the rest of the poem went. Keats was really inclined to be a bit gutless, anyway, so I switched to Pope and intoned, 'Know then thyself, presume not God to scan, the proper study of mankind is man,' and was able to continue for seven or eight more lines before my memory let me down once more.

Miss Rookes said, 'Was that you singing in the bathroom again this morning, Robert?' as I put the breakfast tray on her bed.

'Yes, I suppose it must have been,' I admitted.

'I didn't mind,' she said. She pecked a little smile up at me, and I grinned back at her, wondering why all women were not like Miss Rookes, who never gave me any worry about sex, or much else, for that matter. She was the nearest to what was, at the moment, my ideal sort of woman on matters of sex: one who never upset a chap's equilibrium.

Mr Robbins was on his back and snoring in a bubbling fashion, his heaving breath was no doubt aerating some large body of liquid in his system. I put down his tray on the chest of drawers and began to listen attentively, anxious to note the characteristics of the noise as information for Harry, but Mr Robbins swallowed his last snore, groaned and sighed as he rolled over on his side in a heave of blankets, with a final explosive sound that was a collector's item of a very different sort.

Before I went back to the kitchen for Mrs Ranier's tray, I went to the bathroom and combed my hair in front of the mirror behind the door, and straightened up my eyebrows with a finger wet from my tongue, and was quite all right until I got into her room. She sat bolt upright and yawned, stretching her arms above her head. The drapes were already pulled back, and a book was face downward on the bed; she must have been reading, and then dozed off again. The stretch and wriggle of her shoulders bobbled her body and she dropped her arms, eyes still shut tight, shivering, as she pushed her elbows into her sides and flexed her arms, leaning slightly forward, spilling against the looseness of her nightdress.

'I was delighted with your football success,' she said, the words tumbling out in her gasp of relaxation, her eyes flying wide open.

I put the tray down, and said, 'I saw you. What were you doing there?'

'Dear me – you're in one of your impolite moods again,' she said, and was so right.

'What were you doing there?' I repeated, as though she had just appeared above the terrace of the football field, and was staring at me.

'I read about the game in the paper, old chap, and you'd told me you played football. It was my afternoon off, and so I thought I'd just go along and see how my young man of the morning performs.'

'You've no right,' I said. 'It's not fair.' I wasn't talking about the football now.

She laughed at me and I lost my head and said, 'Shut up,' and turned away, about to clear out of the room, away from her.

'Wait,' she said in a sharp tone, and when I looked back at her she had one hand out, quite the tough schoolmistress. She went on, 'Now look, young man – you'd better explain yourself.'

I looked dumbly at her slender hand. Her fingers were almost as long as pencils.

'I'm sorry for laughing at you, Robbie. I couldn't help it. I'm sorry for going to watch your blessed football.' She waggled her hand. 'Now it's your turn to be sorry.' Her hand was thin and white to the roundness of her wrist, and her arm was a deepening white past the sharp edge of the elbow, where the roundness of her shoulders began. 'Come on, Robbie – don't tell me you're sulking.'

'It's not that,' I said. She simply didn't have enough on for me: the top of her nightgown was inadequate to hide the swells and hollows and shadows and the increasing depth of her flesh. My eyes dragged past her shoulders, filled with one shuddering glimpse of the deeps of her body and rose timidly to the level of her firm gaze. That was always the trouble with my anger with Mrs Ranier: it took me to the heights of courage and then evaporated, leaving me to crawl back down the best way a coward could find.

'It's not that,' I said.

She dropped her hand to the bed. 'Come around and talk to me for a minute.' As I moved slowly back, she went on, 'What a dreadfully solemn face – have I really insulted you?'

My toes turned hard down into my shoes, my shoulder and neck muscles tightened. 'It's not that,' I said.

'Heavens! What are you talking about?' Her face was flickering impatience.

My left arm rose of its own accord and I dared not follow its path. 'You,' I whispered. 'That.' I could not be sure, but my finger-tips tingled; they may have brushed some part of her. 'Down there,' I heard myself say. 'I can't help seeing.'

'Gracious me . . . Ro-o-bert.' She took my wrist and pulled my arm. 'Sit down you blessed boy.' Her eyes had narrowed and her lips were twitching. 'So you're a puritan – I should have guessed.' Her whole face was filled with colour, as though blood was stirring just beneath her skin: she looked much younger than she usually did. 'Come on, sit down, and we'll talk about it.'

I had no choice but to obey her. 'I'm not used to it,' I said. 'I . . . I . . . well, you know.'

'My dear boy – you can get used to me then. You *are* a little idiot. You mustn't be frightened of women.'

My eyes dropped downward, whereupon she folded her arms and straightened slightly. I recovered my eyes and looked into the warmth of her face, and said, 'I'm blushing.' She did not reply, so I mumbled, 'Do you think I'm unhealthy?'

She gave one of those extraordinary smiles (so wide and white and red) that somehow caused the tip of her nose to flatten. 'Of course I don't, Robbie. Look at

81

me as much as you like to, and remember I'll never mind. I can't help looking like a woman and you can sit and talk to me in the mornings, as long as it is all straight between us.'

I rubbed my burning cheeks. 'Don't be contemptuous of me, Mrs Ranier, because I've never had a sister, you see. I've often thought it wasn't natural for me not to have a sister. I wouldn't really let women upset me. I mean I would take all that for granted and be mature,' I said, nodding down to her folded arms.

'Look, I'll show you.' She raised her right hand to the opposite shoulder, which she dropped as though she was about to slip the strap down.

'No.' I grabbed her arm and pulled it away, hard down across her knees. Her surprised gasp increased my fright, but I released my grip.

'Don't be rough on a lady,' she said.

'You scared me. I'm sorry.'

She looked down at her arm and rubbed it. 'Look,' she said, now holding it out. 'You young cave-man.' Just above the wrist there were bloodless indentations outlined in scarlet, and above these marks was a small scratch of my fingernails. I felt like bursting into tears. But she smiled, again with that curious twitch of lips: she wasn't ugly, yet she wasn't far from it. 'You are more solemn than ever – I'm really a bad teacher,' she said. 'It serves me right, throwing you into a panic like that.'

'I'm extremely sorry.' I gripped my hands together on my knees. There were slight smudges of dirt under my thumbnails, so I buried my thumbs under my hands. My legs looked thick and coarse-skinned: I was an overgrown lout.

She patted my arm. 'Please, please don't feel badly;

it is all my fault. I suppose I had forgotten my sense of what . . .' She paused, now holding my arm lightly with her fingers. 'Really, I've forgotten what I have forgotten. One can't forget more thoroughly than that, you must admit.'

My eyes were prickling, no matter how much I blinked them. 'It's me, Mrs Ranier – all of a sudden I am having trouble growing up,' I said.

'I'll help you, old man – and don't worry about it.'

'Everything you say or do to me is teasing – I'm just beginning to realise that.'

'Then you tease me right back.' She patted my arm. 'I'm a lonely old thing, Robbie, hidden away and brooding. You're good for me, in a silly way, so don't take offence so much at what I say.'

'I like you, really. The other thing is not your fault.'

'You can get used to it.'

'It would help, I suppose.'

'Don't think that there's anything wrong, old boy – I can see that pure heart on your sleeve.'

'That's a nice way of saying I'm backward.'

'No, it's not. Get that idea out of your mind once and for all. Please.'

This gentleness of her voice made me ache with relief: there was no doubt, I felt then, that here was a good friend: she really did like me, for some strange reason of her own: she, who was mature, and a woman. I shifted my position on the bed so that I could face her more easily, and my relief was a sensation of breath at the back of my throat: I had to open my mouth and huff it all out with a jerk of my head. And then I grinned at her.

'Gosh, once or twice lately, I've been able to almost feel myself growing up,' I said.

4

The chill and wind left the valley and what remained
of winter passed into spring. The Albertville district
becomes green with grass in the spring; for that matter,
the earth of most of the North Island becomes a warm
cud of grass, and rubbed in the hand it moistens and
the moisture is like the juice of grass; when it rains
this earth yeasts with grass, the hills are softened by
it, the land grows lush and the air tastes of it, the sky
reflects and the people are blinded by it. But this
particular spring there was probably nothing quite as
green as me.

I tried to tell Margery about Mrs Ranier this night
after she had beaten me at chess once again. Even
though I was sure she would go through life swapping
this for that, once she was sure of ultimate advantage,
I refused to brood over a game when I had somebody
like Mrs Ranier to worry me stiff. So I mentioned Mrs
Ranier to Margery, and all she asked was, 'How old
is she?'

'Over thirty,' I answered.

That was practically that, as far as she was concerned. There were only a couple of questions left
now.

'What does she look like?'

So I tried to put my impressions of Mrs Ranier into
some sort of order, the refrigerator motor snapped into
life and the subdued rumble erased the disturbing
outline of her body in my mind, and I became aware

of the kitchen, where Margery and I had played so
many games of chess in the past winter months: in
such a place – with the long chrome sink and the
squares of cupboards above, the bulging gas stove
that was almost as cool and white as the refrigerator,
the rows of plates, cups, saucers and dishes in pastel
displayed on shelves along the far wall, the dull red
of the linoleum on the floor – in such a place, a woman
like Mrs Ranier simply could not exist, even in the
mind.

'What does she look like?' I repeated. 'I don't know.
She's like any other woman, I suppose, except for her
hair, which is red.'

'What sort of clothes does she wear?'

'Clothes?' I was surprised. 'How on earth would I
know. Clothes, that's all.'

Margery slid off her chair to her knees so that only
her head was showing above the table. 'Come on now –
tell me what I'm wearing.'

While I stared at her, my surprise increasing, she
rolled her head to one side, and with an obvious effort
induced about three wrinkles to appear on her forehead. 'If you can tell me the colour of my dress I'll
give you some of Mum's pavlova cake for supper.'

I took the chess board in my two hands, jumped to
my feet and, leaning across the table, brought it down
on her head. She squealed and dropped out of sight.
'You're wearing old flour-bags,' I cried, 'and you look
like something the cat brought in.'

A tentative plucking at my legs gave me only brief
warning that she had crawled under the table. Her
second grasp, this time at my ankle, was more suc-
cessful and, in trying to jump away from the threat
of her other reaching hand, I lost balance and fell

sideways on the floor. The breath bumped out of my body with the force of a whale-spout.

'Are you all right?' she asked, the burning suns of her cheeks moving across my dim sight.

I sat up slowly and folded my arms about my knees. 'You ought to be more careful,' I said. 'I could have broken my neck.' Now able to take a deep breath, feeling immediately better, I said, 'You beat me at chess with your rotten tactics and then you slam me to the floor. It's a bit tough on a man.'

This night I kissed her three times: once in the kitchen, quickly, when I was helping her make a cup of tea, and we were still fooling with each other, and twice when I was leaving, beside the gate in the shadow of the garage. The front door was open, and the hall light beamed out across the concrete steps to the lawn; the windows of the lounge, where Mr and Mrs Blake were sitting, spilled out more light across the path; I had a sense of great daring. These two kisses were quite long ones, and hard enough to hurt my lips.

2

I certainly wasn't going to expose myself again to Harry about Mrs Ranier. The nearest I got to talking to anybody else about her was this morning I opened the door of Mr Robbins' room and found him awake for the first time in weeks. Hesitating at the sight of blood-streaked eyes blinking out of the twilight between blankets and pillow, I whispered 'good morning' knowing how sensitive this man was to sound.

'Is it, old boy?' Mr Robbins' voice carried a spluttering ring, as though it was issuing from the neck of a bottle.

'It is, sir. Very good morning as a matter of fact. Where would you like this?'

'On the dressing table, please.'

Carefully pushing a soiled white shirt aside, I put the tray down. Mr Robbins cleared his throat with a couple of rasping growls, sighed, and heaved about in his bed.

'Saw that red-haired woman in the passage last night. Damned striking piece of goods, I must say. What's her name, again?'

'Mrs Ranier, Mr Robbins.'

'All up front and nothing behind,' he muttered. 'They seem to build them that way nowadays.'

'Yes, sir.'

Mr Robbins pushed the blankets to expose a yellowed, crumbling face that looked on the verge of total collapse until his fumbling hand groped, found and inserted the vital support of his false teeth. Then the underlids of his eyes twitched, his jaw moved jerkily, and a partial restoration of the ruin was made.

'In my young day you never knew what a woman was like until you really got down to it, if you could, but nowadays they go flouncing around and it's there for everybody to see.'

I had been about to move out the door, but now I paused and answered, 'You mean when you were young you did not have to worry about how women looked at all?'

'What's that?'

'I mean they would be all dressed up from neck to ankle, with hoop skirts and all that, so young chaps would never have the slightest worry about women or girls.'

Mr Robbins barked out laughter. 'That's what you think, young fellow m'lad. We worried about 'em all the time, by God.'

'What I mean is, you would not have to worry about what you saw?'

'Dammit, boy, it was what we couldn't see that worried us. Never could tell whether a woman had a wooden leg or a bosom made entirely of whalebone or something like that.'

'Oh.'

Mr Robbins propped himself up on his elbow and glared at me. 'There was the story of the fellow who married a girl and waited on their wedding night for her to take off her bustle, only to discover she didn't wear one.'

'I don't see——'

'What she had sticking out behind was backside, all backside, boy.'

Mr Robbins had dropped back to his pillow and was still gargling moist splutters of mirth, as I left the room.

3

I never gave my step-mother a chance.

'What do you think of Mrs Ranier?' she asked over the tea table.

'She's not very friendly at all, really,' I said. 'But she seems all right, I suppose.'

'I don't like her la-di-da ways,' my step-mother said. 'She's quiet, though, and pays a month in advance.'

88

'That's a help,' I said, not giving a thing away.

'Another thing – she's untidy,' she said, and I laughed at her, all in good fun, and she dropped her head back and tossed a hand at me, saying, 'G'on with you,' and laughed with me, because an hour before I had found all the dry washing in a pile under the window and had folded it myself, rather than let it stay there, while she got on with the vacuuming, which should have been done in the morning, anyway.

We liked each other, my step-mother and I, and perhaps one day I will come to love her. But I was definitely a young man who lacked a father to kick him in the backside occasionally.

One of these Saturday nights I came home and saw light under the kitchen door. I went along and found her sitting in a chair, beside the scrubbed bare boards of the table. A glass was on the table. The bottle of gin would be in the usual place beside the bread tin in the cupboard under the sink. She was dozing, the concertina in her lap, her hands still under the straps at each end of it. Her head was a mass of those metal curlers, the slack hang of her arms hunched her shoulders, the grey cardigan she wore over her old blue dress pulled high up on her back; she looked a misshapen figure in that slump, which pressed the considerable mound of her upper body down on the loose fullness of her stomach. The curlers glinted under the electric light. Her breathing was a soft rasp.

'Here,' I said loudly. 'Wakee, wakee.'

Her head jerked as she snorted awake and her eyes when she opened them, these eyes of whitish blue, gave no sign of immediate sight: she was pretty bad. Then she saw me, and jumped, a wheezing squeak of air blurted from the concertina, and she said, 'Aah –

y'did startle me, boy.' The brogue was there, you see.

'Begorrah and bejabbers I did, did I?' I said.

'Aah,' she laughed, dazed, but putting her head back, waiting for her good nature to catch up, I suppose.

'Would ye be liking me to dance a little jig for ye, Missus O'Flaherty?'

She pulled the concertina against her waist and laughed again.

'Ah now, Missus – come on with the music, and we'll be having a grand Irish night of it. Would ye be playing please?'

My voice rose much higher than I had intended, and perhaps my face didn't look any too pleasant to her. Anyway, she realised that I wasn't joking the same instant that I realised it myself, and we stared at each other, appalled, each waiting for the other to pretend that nothing had happened. But my anger had tricked me, and left me exposed, as much to myself as her, and I could do nothing then.

'You're so like your father,' she said.

'I can't help that,' I answered. 'There's nothing wrong with it, either.'

'New Zealand is full of snobs, and you're a New Zealander,' she said. 'That you should say that, boy.'

She was getting into a paddy, obviously, and I had to make some kind of effort: 'I'm sorry – it wasn't like that at all.'

'You're all the same, not being yourselves.' Her voice was shrill, and her full cheeks tight, and all the drowse burned away from her eyes.

I said, 'I really meant it about a couple of tunes.'

'Find out what you are, boy, and like it, and don't be ashamed of your kin.'

'But I want you to play,' I cried again.

'Play I will, and ye'll listen,' she shouted. 'Sit down and listen.'

I pulled out a chair from behind the table and sat down. She was in her temper, young with it, the signs were obvious: the flickering memory of bright blue eyes, and tossed black hair: a flickering, and no more, through bulges of flesh, and under a cluster of hair-curlers, over the dummy body of age.

She glared at me across the bare table with a single empty glass on it, pushed her chair back and crossed her legs, to offer a high knee to that scuffy little con-certina. I was not frightened of her temper, which was always a quick storm that cleared the air of any un-pleasantness, but of my response to her challenge: despite my attempt at conciliation, I really wanted to mock her again. Desperate, I laughed, and said, 'Let's wake the whole house,' and slapped my hands together, careful not to look at her in case she knew. The meat-dish was upturned on the gas stove in the grease-splattered and blackened alcove beside the sink which was stacked with unwashed dishes: we sat at the table under a single unshaded light, fly-stained, in the big kitchen of ancient cupboards, heavy crockery and an ironing board that was always down: she squashed out her alien tunes, and I listened, trying very hard not to be what I was and to know what she was. Soon she began to enjoy herself, humming to her own play-ing as she kept softening eyes on me. I was determined to hear her out, and I did, and when she wept a little I could even feel that way myself. But her tears were shed because she was Irish and sentimental, while my damp eyes were because I was a New Zealander and, presumably, a snob.

In my defence it could be said that there were quite a few chaps my age who were ashamed of one or both of their parents. Harry, for instance, was quite humble about his father because he was only five feet six inches high, had missed the first world war, been too old for the second, and now worked at the gasworks.

5

Despite my best efforts, and her decency about it all, the sight of Mrs Ranier often worried me, even when we were talking about the most serious subject of all, her husband George. She always spoke of him with that careful language that suggested previous use on the same subject. George's face, she said, was an unruffled surface of tanned, smooth skin over a nice mind: he was born to a happy childhood, untroubled in adolescence and imperturbable in adulthood. She had him polished and wrapped like that, you see.

'He sounds quite all right to me,' was all I could manage. After all, George was a New Zealander.

'He is extremely dull.' Her bitterness did not disturb her face any more than the wing-flaps of a sea-bird could ruffle the surface of an ocean; she spoke so flatly that she might have been reading aloud – at least the way I would have spoken if I had been reading aloud. In the bedroom at the corner of the house we seemed far away from the reality of her past, I was sitting on the edge of her bed with only this slight usual worry on my mind, and she was propped against the pillows with folded arms, and outside, through the open window, with the vague glimmer of stockings on a coat-hanger on the raised sash, the deep green of the rhododendrons banked away from the hedge, and the wall of the neighbouring house was a shield behind which the whole world kept its distance. It was hard to think of her room as untidy, even though there was a scattering of small unrecognisable bottles and boxes on the dresser, and magazines and books were higgledy-piggledy on the bedside table, leaving little room for the tray; invariably, too, her blue candlewick dressing-gown flopped anywhere about the end of the bed, high-heeled shoes were dropped carelessly in a line beside the duchess, and clothes (among them, I was sure, underwear) were usually tossed on the easy chair between the duchess and the bed, on the opposite side to where I was, the shadowed and mysterious side. I was only too pleased to let that side stay a mystery.

Did George mind it very much when she divorced him? I asked, forgetting that I shouldn't ask silly questions. Now, for once, the barest suggestion of disturbance tickled her face. 'Ah, dear me, Robbie – it was George who divorced me. You have it the wrong way around.'

'Oh, you mean he got fed up with you, too.'

'Yes.' She shook her head slowly. 'I was a very naughty girl, and in his patient way he finally decided to get rid of me. Not that I minded, of course.'

'Don't you have to do something before anybody can divorce anybody else?'

'That's right.'

'Well, how on earth could anybody divorce you?'

'I did something.'

'What did you do, then?'

She sighed. 'Dear me, now you want to know all the awful things about me.'

'Not if you don't want to talk about it – I thought you did, y'see.'

She put her hands under the blankets and pushed herself up against the top of the bed, and I had trouble

94

with my eyes again. 'I went out with other men,' she was saying. 'That's pretty bad.'

'Did you?' I was surprised at the bang-banging of my heart; I had thought I was at least past all that.

'I behaved very, very badly. Even the judge said so.'

'Oh, well.' The strange thing was that she was decent as could be: she was wearing new floral pyjamas now, that were really quite substantial, and not transparent like the silk lace stuff, even if the design was the same.

'Everybody said so.'

It had been the movement underneath, the sudden definition of curving shape that had been created and destroyed by the effort of pushing herself back. I decided that the fact that my attention had been claimed was not remarkable, nor a sign of lingering immaturity. After all, I looked at her lips and eyes more than once, and found them of continuing interest, and they were in full view.

'Are you disgusted with me?' she said. 'You look quite depressed.' To reassure her, I immediately gave my views on married women going out with other men: anybody had a right to be friends with anybody, I told her, and nobody had a right to say to anyone that they should not be friends with anybody else. It was no use being married if it stopped you from doing what you wanted to do. For the first time, I believed that Mr Ranier must have been a dull chap. 'I see it now,' I added, 'he was not of your mental calibre: that was the trouble.'

Hesitating on the brink of further speech, she regarded me with that strange look I had come to regard as deep friendliness: a swimming softness filled her eyes and the queer set of her face relaxed for a quivering instant, as though she might be about to burst into tears, and yet that twitch of her lips finally turned into a smile. 'Bless you,' she said.

'Again?' I said, 'You are always blessing me.'

'That's right,' she added. 'You might even be right, Robbie, because – despite everything – I have come out of the mess with a certain moral advantage, because dear George wants to forgive and forget, to start all over again.'

'But it's too late now, isn't it?'

'Yes,' she said. 'I suppose it is too late.'

2

There was sunlight in Mrs Ranier's room this morning. It gave me the idea about the beach, which I used to cover up my embarrassment. She was sitting there telling me of how she enjoyed a sense of hibernation in Albertville. 'I like to think I am a special brand of village idiot,' she said, as I perched on the side of the bed.

'It sounds lonely.'

'A few hours a day in the bookshop gives me a little to think about,' she said. 'And three or four minutes' chatter with you each morning helps, like washing my face and hands in cold clean water before returning my mind to its cave.'

'You mixed that up a little,' I laughed. 'You really can't help pulling my leg can you?'

'A pull of the leg, a kiss of the hand – it is all the same to you. And the cave reference fits, because I like to think I'm something of a hermit as well.'

'Not many hermits have got a double-bed,' I said, nodding at the width of her bed, hardly disturbed by her night's sleep: the stretch of her legs underneath the covers were like moulds in a plaster smoothness: she certainly was a tidy sleeper.

'As I say, Robbie, it is an unfriendly bed.'

'I've never heard of an unfriendly bed before. With you in it, of course, it seems an extraordinarily friendly place to me.'

These lines of her face flickered and she straightened and bowed, coming right forward, and I was confronted by a view of my old troubles again, and my blush was as hot as it had ever been on my cheeks. She noticed this as she sat back, and said, 'Oh dear, I forgot,' and I was sure there was contempt in her voice.

Looking away from her, desperate, I saw the sunlight, and said, 'You ought to go to Raggleton Beach on an afternoon off. It's great out there, and the weather's getting hot, y'see,' and I kept right on talking about the beach and its attractions. Even while I was thinking how much I deserved her contempt for still being a gawky fool despite the help she had given me.

'I've heard enough, Robbie,' she interrupted, 'I'll see this glorious beach of yours soon, I promise you.' She sounded kind and friendly, but there was contempt still lurking in the adult regard of her wide blue eyes.

But she had really listened to me about the beach, I discovered this next morning, after I had explained the peculiar way that Mrs McFarlane, the mathematics teacher, was wearing her hair. (I did not explain that Robert Dawson, who was an expert on sex and allied subjects, reckoned it had something to do with her pregnancy.) When I was showing her how short Mrs McFarlane had cut her hair, I actually brushed her shoulder with my hand, and she stirred and said, 'It is worse than smoking.'

'I didn't know you smoked.'

'I don't. But I used to. It took me months before I could really give it up. And even then I could not resist occasionally lighting up and taking the first puff, and then I had to throw the whole cigarette away.'

'It sounds very trying.'

'When I see somebody smoking now, I still feel like smoking, and if I'm tipsy I actually will smoke and to blazes with it.'

'Anyway Mrs Ranier – what's worse than smoking?'

'Put your hand back on my shoulder, old son.'

I rubbed my hand on my shirt, and put it carefully on her shoulder. She turned away her head quickly, her hair flicking over my wrist.

'Your hair tickles.'

'I feel like smoking,' she said. 'Take your hand away.'

And then, with the same abruptness with which I had changed the subject the morning before, she said, 'Would you like to take me out to this Raggleton Beach of yours this afternoon?'

'Eh?' I recovered myself. 'Go swimming, you mean? I . . . there's school . . . Oh, you mean I should skip school? Gosh!'

'It's just an idea, that's all. I'm not working.'

I took one of my deepest breaths ever. 'A jolly decent idea, Mrs Ranier. I'd be awfully glad to skip school, too, because it is virtually finished, regardless.' I screwed up my eyes carefully. 'I have skipped school on occasions before, y'know.'

Actually the last time I had played truant was with Harry, when we were eight years old, and Bettsy Horner had told on us.

This sky was a white-hazed blue. It was a sweltering
day. I went across to Victoria Avenue after lunch
carrying my leather school-bag under my arm, confident in my being as well-groomed as possible, having
spent five minutes in the cloakroom before leaving
school on washing my face, wetting and combing my
hair, and scratching my finger-nails clean with a paper-
clip. On reaching the avenue I slowed for a moment
and, on looking towards the bridge, nearly lost my
nerve. My feet padded rather than rapped: either the
bitumen of the pavement was heat-soft, or I was
treading very timidly. The whole town was as quiet
as my feet, as though the shimmering heat ripples were
muffling all sound. There were no people under the
shaded length of the shop verandahs, but the glaring
windows of the shops I was passing hid dark interiors
where, I was sure, people were watching me. The
effort to keep my legs moving became too great, so I
stopped and wiped my forehead with the back of my
hand. This gesture brought everything to life: a tram
rattled past, a woman pushing a pram appeared out
of a nearby doorway, a telegraph boy cycled by,
whistling drowsily, and, farther down and in the
middle of the avenue, in the wavering air of the heat,
the squat bodies of men took vague shape. I resumed
walking, sure that she would not be where she said
she would be, so that there was nothing to worry
about, really. The men in the avenue became council
labourers, filling in pot-holes around the tram-lines
outside Woolworths. Bubbling whiffs of boiling tar
tainted the thick warmth of the air.

She was the cool, adult woman at the corner of

Seddon Street, her hair tight in some kind of a knot at the back of her head, her skin stale milk-white, apparently not as lined as usual, her blue eyes clear and not particularly friendly at my approach. She was wearing a white blouse with brown buttons that tumbled like pennies to a green belt that clipped around the top of a light brown skirt, which was almost the colour of the large leather bag she had looped over her arm. Buttons, skirt, bag: they matched; I would let her know that I noticed these things. Her flat-heeled shoes, more like sandals than shoes, actually, were brown, and her legs unstockinged. She was right for summer, I supposed.

'Greetings,' I said, smiling at her. But her eyes were cool and she did not smile back. She nodded her head down Seddon Street and said, 'The bus stop is down there?'

'Yes.' I was surprised, and would have asked her what the matter was, but she moved on down the street without another glance at me, before I could speak, and had nearly reached Todman's Garage before I was able to catch up with her. She was quite tall, I noticed for the first time: almost up to my ear, and I had only four or five inches to go before reaching six feet. Out of the hot darkness of the garage mouth came the whoop of a man, presumably emitted at the sight of her. There must be a lot of men of that calibre working in garages.

'A great day,' I said.

'Yes.'

My short trousers among all the longs in the street, a school-bag under my arm where there were men puffing away at cigarettes – I was probably looking too much like a schoolboy altogether for one of her years.

A few minutes' conversation over her breakfast tray in the morning might well be a different kettle of fish from wasting a whole afternoon on somebody who was dressed like a blasted juvenile.

'If you'd rather not go to the beach, I don't mind,' I told her.

'Of course I'm going.'

I was about to ask whether she wanted to be bothered with me tagging along, when a surge of pleasure smothered my apprehension; that she was treating me in an aloof and disinterested manner became pleasing and I did not mind that she was silent for the few minutes that we waited at the bus stop, that when she boarded the bus ahead of me she said to the driver, 'Two, to Raggleton, please,' dropping a half-crown on the wooden tray for two punched tickets, and then saying, 'You take the change, Robbie,' and marching on down the bus leaving me, a little boy to take the sixpence from the driver. I should have been insulted, I knew, but it did not matter: being with her was enough. I would give her the sixpence back sometime, cracking a joke that would make her recognise that she had behaved like a big sister.

The Shamrock Hotel, on the other side of the railway line, was the edge of the town. Past there, the road hugged the bank of the river, clean and shining through the droop of the weeping willows. At the very point where the willows ended, a swinging curve of the river lowered the bank into a silted desolation of gorse and manuka scrub, and the road had to turn to the right to the higher ground a mile to the north, before it could turn back towards the coast. Wooden milkstands, as regular as milestones, marked the route

101

across a strip of dairy country, where heavy-uddered cows chewed their cuds and stared across slack wire fences. She looked out of the jolting window, silent, a cobweb line from the corners of her eyes and mouth occasionally deepening, as though at some abrasion of thought. It did not matter, really. A few more miles and we reached a straggle of houses on the outskirts of Raggleton, and then the verandahs of grimy shops, like the old hands of old men shielding their eyes from the sun, sprang up on each side of the bus.

We got out at the Post Office, two storeys of dull brick, and she gazed about her and commented that it was a frightful little town, so run-down and dirty, and what on earth was that smell? That was the freezing works, near the wharf.

'There are only the beaches on each side of the peninsula that make the place attractive,' I had to apologise. 'There's nothing to see about Raggleton.'

She moved up the main street, letting me be the little boy tagging along, trot-trot. In another second, I thought, she might take my hand to steer me across the street. Just as I was beginning to care, I remembered that she preferred to be a hermit during the day, that she thought of herself as being in hibernation, and I was comforted by the notion that she was ignoring the whole world, not just me. It was a test of our friendship, surely, that I took no offence at her aloofness.

Though she was a stranger here, she sensed the direction of the beach, and walked quickly to the cross-roads, her head high, as though the smell of the freezing works was much worse than it was, and turned down the lane that ran towards the dunes, first past the rotting board fences of a few shacks, and

102

then through the lupins, where the going was sandy, and the sea murmured close.

My school-cap cupped over the back of my head like hot iron, and the rub of the neck of my shirt was chafing. Yet she looked cooler in the baking glare than she did in the dimness of her bedroom: her hair had lost that fire-glow and become yellow, while her lips and eyes alone retained their full definition in the strong sunlight, for her skin was a soft and coarsened blur over her peculiar features. I kept my head half-turned to study her as we walked along, confident in her remoteness of mind, and was surprised when she grimaced and said, without looking at me, 'Have I got a shiny nose?' I tried to laugh away my embarrassment, and said, 'Your eyes are different, that's all,' and looked straight ahead to the sea. There was not much use pretending: I was getting on her nerves.

The sea was calm this day, a deeper blue than the sky, but hazing in the distant height, so that the horizon was indistinct, and the impression of blue, from the shoreline all the long way to infinity, was overwhelming. The tang and the sound of the water's salt smell and frothing slap on hard sand, the gentle rub of island and sea at peace together: it was all there, and I felt it, and was made easier by it, being a pig islander. The beach was a slate smoothness of sand licked by the sea into a shallow curve of a couple of miles from harbour bar to cliffs. Except for a strip of coarse grass that edged the sand along part of the seafront road, it was backed by a wilderness of lupins and marram grass, blue-green and brown where the dunes sprawled against banks of sand and clay.

The dressing shed was at the far end of the grass strip. MEN: the word was painted at one side of the wall, above a heavy black arrow that indicated an entrance. WOMEN: the other word at the other side above another arrow to the opposite entrance: the shed, under the tin roof, was concrete-floored, and divided by several thicknesses of plywood that could segregate the sights but not the sounds of undressing. Because I could hear her moving about on the other side, I hurried, whistling softly to disguise the noise I was making: but it was not possible to stop thinking of the actions that were associated with her sound, so I whistled much louder. My swimming shorts on, I jammed my clothes and shoes and socks into the schoolbag and hastened outside again.

My skin was already warming to the sun as I stretched up and down on my toes to bunch the muscles of my calves and thus emphasise the strength of my legs, regretting once again that there were not at least a few hairs on my chest. Still, the afternoon looked like being all right for me, even in the rôle of little brother, and I could enjoy the resin scent of the pine trees on the opposite side of the seafront road, behind the shuttered tea-rooms that carried the sign, bright-painted in readiness for another summer, 'Ice Cream – Soft Drinks.' In a week or so, the place would be open every day, instead of only at the weekends: I was thinking that I would like some ice-cream if the place were open when she emerged from the other end of the shed, nearly naked. My chest hurt as though my ribs were collapsing. Her costume was two clinging swathes of orange nylon: the thrust and fullness of her bosom was separated and shaped, its covering seeming no more than a blush of the skin, while her shorts were V-shaped and exposed her thighs half-way to her waist, exaggerating the milky length of her legs.

'Gracious,' I gasped, 'nobody wears bathing costumes like that around here.'

'Don't they?' she replied, sounding as though she could not care less about that. She moved on past me, swinging her leather bag to the awkward rhythm of her barefoot walk. Her mid-riff, blending with the oval top of her stomach, loosened and tightened to her movement; I was not sure, but her navel might have been showing. 'We'll camp much farther down the beach, and nobody will be offended by the sight of me, then.' She stepped off the grass and wriggled her feet into the sand, frowning. There was no doubt in my mind that I had annoyed her by my adolescent reaction, and I was about to offer some kind of apology when, with no sign of any thought for me, she walked on down the beach, to where the lupins and marram grass fingered for the sea over the humped slopes of the dunes, and the sky and water were merged in a shimmering haze. I purposely kept a couple of paces behind her, allowed my eyes to move from her heels to her neck and back again, knowing that I had to get accustomed to her to survive the afternoon with dignity: it was not unreasonable of her to have expected that I would be well past goggling at her body now that we were such friends.

The hanging slope of her shoulders moved in contradiction to her hips in a disharmony of movement that made her walk so distinctive. She looked incredibly young, for somebody with a rather old face; her long, smooth legs made the difference. For some reason, I had expected that her legs would look old, too. The slender lines of her back arching up from the snub of her rump was a surprise: it seemed a very slight stem to carry such a heavy fruit, or even to support the width of her shoulders. Then it occurred to me that I knew little about the female body, and it might well be that their shoulders carried the weight in front. I had expected her bottom to be bigger, too; instead, it could hardly match the width of her shoulders, even though it was rounded and full. Margery's would have looked quite big indeed beside it. The line of her hips was slightly angular where they joined her legs – again I was amazed at the length and colour of her legs, so hairless and smooth, as if they had been lacquered, and long-tapering to tiny knees, filling again in flattened curves to neat ankles and small feet. All her extra height was in her legs, that was certain.

She turned up the beach, looked at me over her shoulder, and said, 'I know you are staring – aren't you ever going to get over that?' with the same casualness that she might squash a sand-fly, and made her way up a small depression between the dunes, to where a solitary pohutakawa cast a cramped shade at the foot of a sloping bank of tangled lupin and toi-toi. 'Here,' she said, 'I won't worry you here.' She dropped to her knees, pulled a towel from her bag and spread it carefully on the sand, away from the shade. Then she lay down, head sideways, away from me, on the towel, arms slack to her sides, palms of her narrow hands upward, and she became as still as a store-window dummy dropped there. I was an object of contempt to her; a bloody fool about bodies.

'I'll go for a swim right away,' I said. 'Watch out you don't get burned by the sun. You look pretty darn pale to me – that's what I was looking at you for.'

I dropped my bag and walked the thirty or so yards to the sea, trying to feel good or bad: it did not matter

106

which, as long as there was something. The salt lick of the water, cool and transparent, was over my legs and arms, then my body, and I became listless and too lazy to swim; I flopped about in the shallows, now on my back with wet face to the spinning ball of the sun, then over to my stomach, sometimes to hold my head right under. I did not really care that she was treating me so badly. Someone my age could be very boring, no doubt, able to say or do nothing to interest her on such an afternoon; a few minutes in the morning was my limit as far as she was concerned, that was certainly it. On top of everything else, I had goggled at her swimming costume, and exclaimed 'Gracious', when women all over the world went like that to the beach, probably. She was, after all, wearing more than I was. It was a pity, I thought, that our friendship had been punctuated by the surprises her body gave me. I rolled over into a sitting position in the water and looked back at her. The sulphur bob of her hair, the plaster white of her back and legs glinted in the heat-ripple between the dunes. She was unmoving, and forgetting: I might as well be a million miles away.

My hands clawed at my sides of their own decision, as I gasped in pleasure at what I could do to her: prove that I was an adult who should be held in higher regard, perhaps even show that she was vulnerable, too. Looking up and down the beach, I saw that we were still alone, that we might as well be on a desert island together, as they say. I twisted to one side and then to the other, and the water surged between the new freedom of my legs as I rolled the shorts down over my knees and feet, and then jerked them into the air, the banner of a new Robert Henderson. Splashing out of the water I looked down at the mound of my

stomach, white in the narrow grip of my hips and
fuzzed at the pit, above the slack of what, after all,
was nothing more private than her mammary glands.
My legs were jolly good, even for a full-grown man.
I would shout out to her – no, by gosh, I would go
up the beach and be near enough to see exactly how
she reacted to the same kind of trick, more or less,
that she played on me. I tossed my shorts down and
ran to her, leaping, laughing, until I was level with
her feet, very conscious of my body. I stopped, puffing
loudly, sand sticking to the wet of my legs. 'Hey,
there,' I shouted, and stamped my feet up and down
and jiggled my hands as she stirred. 'Look at me.'
Dazed, she twisted over to her side, raising a hand to
shield her eyes from the glare. I snapped straight,
almost to attention, expanding my chest, waiting for
her eyes to clear. 'It's only me,' I said.

Her eyes, blue-heated reflections of the sky, widened
with a jerk of her yellow head, and her mouth widened,
too, and her shoulders, with a jolting hunch, lifted with
the movement of her head as she gasped in her breath.
I was still for just one clear second of her gaze, and
then turned on my heels and sprinted back to the
water, sand flying from my feet, laughing, in shouts
for her to hear, skittering about like a little boy who
has climbed out of his bath and run away from his
mother. She had gasped; she had been shaken. I
swooped to pick up the swimming shorts with a clutching hand, and waved them above my head and made
leaping strides into the sea. Not till deep water did I
turn and push my shoulders back against the swell.
She was sitting bolt upright, stiffly, I saw at first glance.
Then the giddy reflection from the water, and the
dimness of my wet eyes in the surf jumbled her shape

into wavering streaks of colour. Leaning over, I almost floated as I squirmed back into the shorts. I ducked my head under the water once, swished back my hair, took a heaving breath and licked the salt taste of my lips. Whatever she felt, or said, or did could make no difference. My incredible action was right – it had brought me back from that point so far away from her consciousness and, more important, made us square.

I walked slowly out of the water and up the beach, not looking at her. It was exactly like walking off a football field after playing a good game in which my side had won.

'There,' I said, stopping a few yards from her, looking right at her. 'That teaches you.' She was sitting, her arms folded, and her face was blank of any expression, as though it was waiting on a decision. I could not help smiling, knowing what she was going through. For the first time, I had beaten her : she was waiting on me to help her. I sat down, suppressing a smile to a mere bend of my lips, wondering whether I should make it more obvious to her that it was costing me some effort not to giggle. She opened her mouth to speak, but hesitated, and her eyes narrowed. The decision had been made. Her whole face twisted even more as it sharpened, and she closed her mouth with a faint huh of breath, but I still could not feel other than glad at what had happened. 'Say something,' I said, trying to sound teasing.

Cutting lines exploded across her face and she said, 'You brat.' She got to her knees and lifted her hands. 'Don't,' I said, bringing an arm before my face. But, instead of striking me, she twisted one arm behind her back, pressing the other across her body, as though she was trying to check its trembling. 'You should be whipped,' she said. Her eyes were hooded by the slow fall of their lids, and her cheeks and lips twitched, and then her temper seemed to unbalance her, for one shoulder dipped and her head fell to the same side and the one arm behind her dropped down and she had to sit back on her heels and dig her elbows hard into her waist. 'Get away from me this instant.'

'Please,' I wanted to say, but the words choked into a mumble.

'Get away,' she cried.

My throat had tightened and my anguish was hard on my face as I rose to one knee, ready to run out of her sight and sound, for ever, when she jerked up to her knees directly before me, no more than a few feet away, and raised her arms from her sides to a stretching level with her shoulders. The ends of her orange bra, like a peeling skin, curled around from behind her, slipping and clinging to the swell of her breathing for an instant, before falling away to expose these parts, loosening to new fullness at their release, deep and strong to tips of yellow above the firm white curve of their descent, still high above her waist. Her eyes unhooded, and it was as if their lids had effected the whole disguise of her feeling, for she laughed and swung her arms to clap her hands together, almost under my nose.

'Stop it,' I called, and clasped my hands over my eyes, twisting away from her, and bending over my knees.

'Ha, my lad, you are not so bold and brave, after all.'

Red streaks erupted across the blackness of my sight as I rubbed the heel of my hands into smarting eyes, knowing I had lost to her again.

'Put it back on please,' I said. 'We are quits now.'

110

There was a scuffle of her feet in the sand and she laughed again, from high above me.

'I really fooled you,' she said. 'You forgot I had been an actress, Robbie.' I knew she must be standing up, looking down at me.

'Put it back on, Mrs Ranier.'

'Why, Robbie, I've just started.'

'Eh?'

There was the faint grit of sand compacting to her walk, and then silence. I waited long enough to take three deep and deliberate breaths, relaxing the pressure of my hands on my face, and parting my fingers as I lifted my head. Perhaps she was already back in her full costume. But she was only half-way to the water and standing still, her hands joined at her jaunted left hip, gazing about her with tilted head as though searching the farthest horizons, the narrow stem of her back twisting from one side to the other, bringing the utmost reach of each side of her body into silhouette in turn. Her fingers plucked at her hip and then pulled away, joined again and parted, this time unlacing and finally undoing the tie of her shorts, which unwrapped across her bottom to the opposite hip and slipped down her thigh. She bent forward and rolled the palm of her hand down the side of her leg, twisting the shorts down to her knee, from where they fell into an untidy loop to the ground. She kicked her foot free and walked towards the sea on tiptoes, the mound of each buttock in clenching rhythm.

I looked away, up and down the beach, behind and around, up to the blinding sky, even. There was nobody else to see her. I slished through the sand on my hands and knees and grabbed my school-bag. Now on my feet, and looking at my feet, I walked towards

111

the water, along the tracks made on my previous trip. Where my trail gradually faded on the firming sand, I slowed. Where the sand was hard and damp, I stopped, and raised my eyes just to the frill of the water. 'Mrs Ranier,' I called.

'Yes, Mr Henderson.' She sounded quite far out.

'I think I'll go home now, if you don't mind.'

The sea brushed towards my feet and retreated again. 'Did you hear what I said?' I called again.

'You can look up, Robert,' she replied, from my left.

When I did look, only her head and bare shoulders were visible as she leaned forward into the water about ten yards out. She stretched her arms in front of her and gently splashed her hands. 'Such a prude, after your own exhibition,' she said. 'I was hoping you would come in and teach me to swim.' She was practically nothing but eyes above the water now, ugly-blue and gleaming under the yellow line of her hair, which was getting wet.

'Look, I'll hide in the lupins for a minute if you'll come out and get into your costume,' I said. 'It's not right, y'know.'

'Nothing doing.'

'Well, I'm going to go home.'

Her hands stopped splashing and she kept her arms underneath the water in a sweeping stroke, swimming. 'You can wait for me at the dressing shed then,' she puffed.

'I might.'

She rested again, floating her outstretched hands. 'I thought you might at least teach me——' An arm flashed out of the water and pointed behind me. 'Is that someone up there?' she shrilled. I swung around at the jump of my heart, searching with panicky gaze the ragged line of the dunes and the banks, and her splashing did not disturb me until it was almost too late. She was right back in the shallows, a bare five yards from where I was standing, and at the instant of my gaze she splashed, about to rise from the water and though I turned and ran down the beach I was not quick enough to avoid a momentary sight of the extraordinary hang of these parts of her body, and the roundness of her stomach, as she pushed up from the water. I was not quick enough to avoid her laughter, either, and as I ran I really began to hate her. I wanted her dead, or something drastic like that.

6

By the time this bus reached the Seddon Street
terminus back at Albertville, I was still hating Mrs
Ranier. She had not followed me off the beach, even
after half an hour, when the bus left from the Raggleton post office. Four women were the only passengers
in this creaking bus. They sat in their fat frocks, not
one of them under about forty, and I looked out the
shuddering window at the cows in the paddocks, and
the way they chewed their cuds, the sun on their
backs, the grass at their feet, and then I looked back
at these women, chewing gossip with the same stupid
contentment, the same warm laziness, and the cows
were far preferable. We passed a little boy sitting on
top of a milkstand: he was all freckles, nostrils and
a grin under a man's ancient felt hat: the driver
honked his horn, he waved, and one of the women
said, 'The dear little chap'. This woman had a middle-
age sprawl that took up most of the double-seat; she
had a face that would have looked better on a man,
but only a woman could look at a boy like an animal
remembering many satisfied hungers.

It was no use blaming myself, either, as I tried to
do as I walked up Victoria Avenue, banging my school-
bag against my leg, muttering, 'You retarded bugger,'
and kicking an empty ice-cream carton out of the way
with a swing of my foot. The avenue was cooler now,
and tired, the workmen outside Woolworths had with-
drawn to the kerbside, where they were drinking tea

out of heavy cups. They were stripped to the waist, sweating grime, still in a stupor of heat and tar; they were strong men working their guts out for women.

This was nearly twenty minutes to four, the end of the last period at school, so I hurried and was waiting inside the entrance to the old block as the dismissal bells were ringing. The mellow bricks, the dry creep of the ivy, the edges of the entrance steps rounded by nearly forty years of feet, all the chalk and blackboard atmosphere hurt like kicks of sad memory, as though I was a visitor from my own future; the corridor rumble and then the whooping clatter, the sudden lilt of energy livening the drowsy air, the swinging bags and the white angles of legs and arms as the chaps spilled towards the entranceway all hurt, too; the cries of 'G'day, Boot', the pleasant eyes of admiration, the deference of boys twisting against the tide of movement to avoid bumping me – this couldn't change anything.

Harry saw me and swaggered his wide shoulders through the mob, his face solid and unafraid. 'Where have you been?'

We walked behind the building, across the paved yard, through the alleyway between the high walls of the swimming baths and one side of the engineering block. This alleyway was as cool and as dark as a morning bedroom. Out into the sun at Liverpool Street, we took a short-cut to our end of the avenue. This street was one of the oldest parts of town, of rotting, stained and tumble-down houses, with fences of iron or wood or unkempt hedges, and yards junked with weeds and rubbish. We stopped under the verandah of the HMV shop at the corner of the avenue; traffic ambled past and a tram came to a halt

115

and was hit by a boarding party of students. Down the avenue was Tony's milk-bar, where girls from school congregated in giggling pairs, their pleated dark gym tunics over white blouses no attraction, their black stockings and white panama hats with black ribbon bands actually repulsive.

'A few more weeks and it will be goodbye to school,' said Harry. 'I'll be sorry in some ways.'

'Have you made up your mind what you're going to do?'

'The Government, I suppose. There's not much else except the civil service and they've got a pretty good superannuation scheme, they tell me.' He levelled a finger at the sun. 'Bang,' he explained, as though he really wished he could shoot it down.

'Why don't you try for University?' I asked, but couldn't care less: what I really wanted from him was help.

'Not me, Roberto. My guts are full of learning, to put it nicely.' He snorted with quick feeling. 'You and I are going to miss out, y'know. It will be at least another twenty years before another war is due, so there's none of that for us.'

A couple of doors away was the red and black chemist's shop, with a window full of make-up sets, toothpaste and patent medicine displays and, in one back corner, an open book with illustrations on opposite pages of the male and female body. Three third-form boys had their noses pushed hard against the plate-glass window and were squinting in their concentration on the book.

'That Mrs Ranier is a rotten bitch,' I burst out.

'What's that again?' Harry was goggling at me.

'Mrs Ranier – I hate her,' I said. 'She's a rotten bitch.'

116

He went on looking and I went on talking – talking
in a kind of weak vomit : my words stuttered and stam-
mered, making little sense, yet heaving out of me in
spasms of anger. I thought 'you're making a fool of
yourself', and hesitated, and then stopped altogether.
This would be when my stupid seventeen-year-old lips
were trembling. Harry was still goggling, incredulous.

'I don't quite get the hang of all this,' he said. 'But,
hell's bells, you look bad.'

I realised that I was on the verge of being a complete idiot, for now he looked away from me, embarrassed, while I wiped my arm over my face, back
and forth, as though my weakness was something that
could be rubbed, rubbed away, and then he shifted
around, his shoulder digging against mine, a prompt-
ing to start walking again. This way he would not have
to look me in the face. The red-bulbed façade of the
Regent theatre gleamed dully in the sun, and a flutter
of sparrows zipped in little shrieks about the neon
sign; little shrieks, like my thoughts.

'What's she done to you?'

Single, startled images of her nakedness twisted in
my mind, but I wasn't going to tell him the real story.

'She – she sneers at me,' I said.

'What about?'

'Everything.'

'You're a funny bloke, Roberto. You've hardly said
a word about her since you went mad about the way
she showed too much of herself. Now you break out,
swearing and cursing about the woman all of a
sudden.'

Although this was not unreasonable comment, it
seemed like it to me then, and I cried, 'You're scared
I might want you to do some dirty work.'

117

He stopped and half-turned to face me. My words had been spoken as soon as they entered my mind, as much a surprise to me as they were to him, and we were looking into each other's eyes in mutual bafflement. Then he frowned with an intensity that spilled lines from his forehead down the side of his nose, around the curve of his cheeks, and into the corners of his mouth.

'You're scared,' I cried again, hitting the side of my fist against his chest.

He shook his head. 'Hold on,' he said. 'You'll bust a valve if you're not careful.'

'You've got to help me do something to her.'

'What?'

'Frighten her,' I said. 'I want to frighten her out of her stupid wits.'

'Right – but calm down, damn it.' He half-shouted this as he grabbed my shoulder and pushed me around, and I did cool off, even as he told me to, after a moment.

'That's a load off my chest,' I said.

'In another minute you would have been frothing at the mouth,' he muttered. 'Talk about these Italians.'

In silence we resumed walking. The heat became unbearable; my breath grew short, my eyes blurred in the heavy simmer of the air; the footpath burned my shoes. There was only one thing to talk about now and, when he did not speak, I had to prompt him.

'You've got to do it smartly,' I said.

'What exactly is her trouble though?' Harry asked.

'I told you – she makes fun of me – that's all. I've just had a gutful, and want to have hell scared out of her. It's important to me.'

'I'll do something, but how am I to get at her? It'll

118

take some thought to fix a trap.'

Thought: a wrinkled tennis ball head of an old man was before my eyes; my heart hurt, and my voice was hard to get out.

'If I got her to the Crown land with me would you use the gun to frighten her?' I asked, and instantly the relief at having got something out of my system – the sheer, unadulterated relief – was almost a physical shock.

Harry gasped, and I was laughing as I turned back to face him: he had halted in his stride, as though stricken by the impact of the incredible. My laughter finally roused him, for he raised a hand and raised it in front of my face with a frowning tic of his head.

'Hell's teeth,' he said. 'You're the one.'

'It doesn't matter – not if you're too scared to put a shot near her stupid head.'

He raised his right hand, index finger cocked, extended his left arm and then dropped his head behind his near hand and squinted. The street dimmed and the buildings wavered into an opaque flatness behind him as he stared with frowning intensity at the imaginary object of his sighting, as though he was exploring all the possibility of his contact with it. As he squeezed his trigger finger into his fist, he frowned again.

'I'll do it,' he said, lifting his head, quite determined. 'Any time it can be jacked up.'

'Tomorrow morning, then,' I said. 'I'll try and get her out there tomorrow morning.'

He looked at me suspiciously. 'How come she'll come out with you like that, and you so wild about her?'

'She's a bit like one of the family now,' I lied. 'I

suppose she's like a big sister who really wants putting in her place.'

I had been swimming at the beach once and caught in a strong under-tow I had to fight hard for a foot-hold in the shifting sand, only to be swept back in the last rip of the sucking water and left in a boiling mass of gritty sand. There was no real danger in such shallows, but the momentary sensation of disaster, even though I was far out of the way of disaster, was a thrill given me very cheaply. This idea to pay back Mrs Ranier was like that, even as Harry and I went on talking about it: if anything goes wrong, it will be an accident, I thought; we would be safe in the shallows.

2

This same night was moonless and black-clouded. The avenue was defined by intermittent street lights that had no more power against the blackness than glints of phosphorous in the Pacific Ocean; the darkness banked and spilled back across the pavements and into doorways, casting deeper shadows around the spiritless glares. The Majestic, where Margery and I had been, and the Regent, at the opposite end of the avenue, could only show a few bulbs of feeble glow; the two milk-bars were open, but their plate-glass brightness would be snapped away soon. Albertville relied pretty heavily on the moon and the stars at night, in the interests of electricity conservation, and when they didn't shine it was too bad. This night the darkness was soft and quiet, the picture crowds were shadowy and low-voiced, and even when the trams swung into the avenue from Quay Street, the rumble of wheels, the clang of bells were hushed, and only when the first tram lumbered past us, rocking full, was there a brief glimpse of a community of people.

Margery tucked her hand under my elbow, pulled herself against me, and then pushed her right hand down the underside of my arm, rubbing her head against my shoulder. This was really the kind of warm night it was. 'A penny for your thoughts,' she said. As a matter of fact, my thoughts had been very black indeed, for the entire evening, despite the celluloid distraction. We were out of the avenue and half-way down Massey Street now. Across the road somebody was putting milk bottles out at the gate. 'A penny's not enough,' I answered, 'the least of my thoughts is worth a small fortune.' It was not so many years ago that Harry and I had sneaked out very early one morning and put a dead tadpole in a bottle of Mr Dwyer's milk, because he would not let us look for a tennis ball we'd knocked over his fence the day before: there were a lot of elderly people like that in Massey Street, for some reason.

'Threepence, then,' said Margery. 'That's my highest bid.' She did not sound as though she really wanted to talk. Old Dwyer had his photograph in the *Herald* next afternoon, with the bottle of milk and the tadpole. The general manager of the River Dairy Company made a ponderous statement outlining all the precautions the company took in bottling milk. 'Harry and I used to play around here when we were kids,' I said, and was about to tell her the story when I remembered that the subject of Harry might not please her. Harry had made a wonderful job of re-sealing the bottle after we put the tadpole in, and was really entitled to all the credit. I looked down at Margery and tightened my grip of her hand, and she squeezed my hand in response and, in a desire to be nicer to her, I put an arm about her shoulder. She put her arm around my waist. As we turned into her street, we swung awkwardly against each other and I turned, and pulled her hard against me. We hugged and then separated. 'Somebody might see us,' she said.

We linked arms again and slowly made our way down the street, into the deepening shadows of Trig Hill. Margery was not wearing a scent, but something more like talcum powder. It was very nice, and the frizz of her hair felt very clean when my nose had been buried in it during that hug. I could not help noticing, too, that the natural smell of her skin was different from Mrs Ranier's: it was much lighter, not as deep and warm, or nearly as noticeable. I was busy hating Mrs Ranier.

The shadow of the hill seemed an extra layer of darkness, making the two yellow-glaring pools of light from the lamps at each end of the street even more futile. We were isolated in blackness, with the feel, warmth and sound of ourselves. I had to stop and she groped her hands about my neck, behind my neck, and we kissed. My comfort was marred by my difficulty in controlling my breathing, and because she was leaning on me I had to shuffle my feet to keep balanced. Nevertheless, it was some consolation that I wasn't afraid of Margery, who was, after all, a woman, too.

'Oh, goodness,' she exclaimed, breathily. 'Life is certainly getting complicated.' She sounded thrilled.

'What do you mean – complicated?' She was still holding her arms behind my neck, as though she wanted me to kiss her again.

'Interesting, then.' Her hands pressed the back of my neck and, with some fierceness, I pushed my head down and gave her the longest kiss we had ever had; we were absolutely jammed against each other. She turned her head away first, and I released her and twisted from her grasp, feeling it was time we started walking again. I was a little annoyed with my breath, too.

'I used to think I would die if you ever kissed me,' whispered Margery.

'Don't you like it?'

She rubbed her head against my shoulder once again as we moved on, and laughed. 'Don't be silly.' And then, as though the darkness had made it possible for her to bare some feeling, she exclaimed, 'You don't say anything, though, Robert.' I felt her actually tremble with feeling as she spoke, and the higher pitch of her voice was quite startling.

'What do you mean?' I became nervous and shook her hand. 'Don't speak so loudly, either.'

Then she actually stamped her foot, and a clap of thunder would not have upset me more. 'You're so silent about it all, Robert Henderson. You should say something before or after, or at least sometime, anyway. Something nice, about how you feel. We've been going on like this for more than a month now, and you haven't said a word to me about it. Not a word.'

'What the——' I choked on the next word in time's nick, not quite bewildered and angry enough to swear. 'Bloody hell,' would have sounded uncouth. But as I wriggled my mouth about in baffled splutters, my mind swept up words and phrases to utter that appalled me. It took some time to assemble a few dignified words together. 'Margery, if you are in any way dissatisfied, please feel free not to go out with me,' I said as steadily as possible. It would take a long time to recover from such outrageous criticism.

'Ro–bert.' Her intonation vaguely reminded me of Mrs Ranier. 'All I meant was that you haven't said anything about . . . about, well, how much you like me, or even if you do, much.'

'It is enough to make me spit.' I said that before I could censor the vulgarisms my mind was erupting again.

'What was that?' At least she sounded anxious.

I wished it was not so dark. To see her, the house, the slow rise of the hill: to see all the familiar sights of the street would help to keep everything right, for there was more than sound and touch being magnified in this blackness of a moonless valley. There was, too, this sense of a need for something, and an ignorance of what it was.

'It's all quite unimportant.' I put as much snap as I could into that, and she moved against me with a snuffle of feeling and flipped her arms around my rigid neck.

'Please,' I said.

'You've been awful all evening,' she was saying. 'Hardly speaking, glaring at me, not caring whether I was alive or dead.'

There seemed nothing else for me to do but pat her and say, 'I've been thoughtful, that's all, and I'm awfully glad I'm out with you.'

She raised her head and the point of her chin was on my shoulder, and somehow or other I also began to feel the warmth of her body. Perhaps it was the way she was holding me, or because our position was different, but even though we were not too close against each other gentle pressure points against my body burned and my back tingled when she held me.

'I don't believe you.' She sounded anxious and her words ended in a whimper of breath against my face and she was standing on tiptoe pecking at me. She had always been an up-and-down sort of person, depressed one minute and elated the next, and she was shaping that way at this, it seemed. Anyway, I was not going to run away from another woman today, so I started kissing her, holding her more tightly, wanting her to be afraid and to cry halt, leaving me open to criticism only for daring and aggressive masculinity. But the intensity of her response surprised me, and I knew I had a job on my hands. I wasn't going to run away, though.

Pushing her away I said, 'Let's sit down somewhere.' I think perhaps I would have liked to have added, 'And think.' But we opened the gate and, hand-in-hand, moved across the lawn, the grass hushing under our feet. My heart was thudding and the air became over-hot, our hands damp. 'On the grass – here,' I whispered, guessing that she was feeling about for the front steps. I pulled her hand and dropped to one knee, and then guided her towards me, whispering, 'We might as well be comfortable.' She seemed awkward and slow. 'Be careful of the steps,' she said. 'We're nearly hitting them.' She bumped against me, half-turned, and I put an arm about her. She must have been trying to sit down, for now she flopped sideways and just for a moment it seemed that she was going to employ a wrestling hold on me for some purpose. Then we settled down and the whole business developed into a kind of race. Her breathing was as loud as mine, and when we rested, cheek against cheek, she was

125

burning hot. I was damned if I was going to talk to her though; it would sound like an admission that her earlier complaint was justified.

We changed position, almost lying down, now. I would show her. I put my hands on to her body, hoping she would frighten, but she did not seem to care. I would have to show her. There was somebody else's laughter in my mind, and my excitement became like an anger; there was nothing I would not do now, she would have to stop me, she, the frightened, inexperienced one. Her gasps, her heat were nothing until she knew what I would do. No matter what happened she had to be the first to want to stop. I wanted to stop, but did not care. There was nothing I would not do, if she did not stop.

Then I simply had to pause, to give her a chance. She was shivering under my hand, and hot, so I shifted my hand and poised above her, a reluctant Casanova, to make her realise that she had to stop. She stirred and sighed, as though challenging me, and at the realisation of my own weakness I grew desperate: there was nothing I would not do to beat her, to make her stop. And I grew fiercer until she twisted and whimpered at my movements. I persisted once more, and at last she gave in. 'No, no,' she moaned, and wrenched sideways. There was a hard bumping crack, and she moaned, louder, in pain this time. 'Stop it,' she cried, frightened at last, clawing at me, even though I had stopped. I jerked myself away, groping for her shoulders to hold her still, to tell her it was all right, and all the while I was seeing her.

Little drops of blood were bursting out of her skin above her forehead, her mouth was blotched and red, open. She was crying out in a daze that was changing

126

to horror. Above the drops of blood appeared a scarlet cut. I could actually see her face like that, and then I saw my hand gripping her shoulder. The bodice of her dress was unbuttoned and the dress itself was crumpled up her legs. She was bright white and gleaming about the tops of her legs and where she was loose from her brassière. The impact of the sight made me cry out, too, and then I turned into the glare of a flashing light that swung above my eyes even as a man's voice roared out from behind it. Then the light swung down. Margery screamed again, and a great weight struck me on the forehead, and her scream wavered and faded.

3

This woman was sobbing in clicking gulps, as though her false teeth were out of control. My feet were loose and something hard was hitting my ankles. There was a clawing ache under my arm. The chattering did not belong to the sobs which were part of another's uncontrolled weeping that rose and fell in groans of hysterical effort. There was an arm about me, with a hand that roughly gripped my flesh under my shoulder. It was the edge of the steps that was hitting my ankles. The woman was sobbing and talking, and it was Margery who was making the other noise. 'Daddy, Daddy,' she was crying. I wanted to laugh into the blackness, because she had become frightened first, and was still frightened, and tried to think of the right words to call out to her, to ask her what else she could expect of a man. The blackness twisted into strands across a light, and there was this other light, this man, this woman. I was leaning through a doorway; light of shining mirrors was glinting and a carpet was moving on a swinging floor. This light was the white bowl on a chain from the ceiling. This was their hall-way. Their place was being tipped over on top of me as I lay on the ground. But there was that arm holding me. Only my legs moved freely, sending my heavy feet scraping sideways against the bottom of the wall.

Now a chair was under me, and it was a new light from a different ceiling above. 'I don't care if I have killed him,' said Mr Blake. It was Mr Blake, of course. Mr Blake made the first light shine down on us. Margery was bleeding about the face in the light: I understood why she could be seen so clearly. Mr Blake was shining a light. The top of Margery's legs were gleaming and the bodice of her dress was crumpled. The blood on her face was gleaming, too.

The black strands were twisting and thinning until there were mere lines across my sight. I strained with eyes wide open and looked at the piano and the scat-tered piles of music on top of it. Margery was really very untidy. The carpet was on a steady floor. This was their lounge, of course. The furniture was cold and empty, as though it belonged to the dark, as I did, for the feel of the light was hard. The familiar things were hateful. This carpet was a slimy vomit of colours, the piano was the pulpy body of a white-scabbed insect, the chintz furniture hollow contortions of evil design. I closed my eyes and found no darkness there: a mouth that was screaming soundlessly was close against my eyes. Then a door slammed open, and the mouth began to fill with audible moans. Never had I heard such a weeping and a wailing.

How long I was there like that I could not know or

care; everything that was going to happen would happen without my participation in any preparation for it.

The thick voice said, 'Blubber away – there's more coming to you yet.'

Because my head was hard against the back of a chair, the convulsive jerks of my neck hurt very much: it was as if the whole weight of my heaving chest was supported by my throat and was strangling me. I pushed up in the chair, pressing my hands hard against my face.

'Here's something to go on with.'

The voice was a distortion of a voice I knew; the words could mean nothing until I remembered who might talk like that. Then my head, the side of my head, jarred, and there was the sound of the whole house shaking, and a weight tumbling. Though I did not know it then, I'd just been handed a fourpenny one from no miserly hand.

Now my body was supported by a solid mass; I was curling up on it, as though I was in bed, nearly asleep. That was it: I was in bed, and had been having a nightmare, which was ending now. Of course I was in bed, and I would wake up to another new and wonderful day in good old Albertville.

The hurt of my head came back, swelling into a thumping pain down one side of my face.

'My God, what have you done to him?' This woman again, screeching. I must not drift back into the nightmare. Wake up, wake up: I tried to say it out loud. Pain must be part of the nightmare, too. Pain and shouting. The voices were louder as I stirred.

'Don't touch him again, Jim. The doctor's coming.'

It had really happened, then. I was on the floor now,

and I had been on the chair. A doctor was coming.
The man was Mr Blake; the woman was Mrs Blake.
The light had shone down and Margery had screamed.
The man had jumped down. Mr Blake was the man.

'He's all right – he's coming around now. Go back to
Marge.' Mr Blake was shouting.

'Promise me you'll leave him alone. Please God,
promise.'

'See to the girl; I'll take care of him. It's on your
head the whole thing, letting your daughter go out at
night, doing what she liked.' The words were lashing
around the room, foamed from a thick mouth.

'Jim, the neighbours have rung for the police.
They're coming, the police, do you hear? The whole
neighbourhood will know what's happened. Jim,
please.'

I opened my eyes. The hem of a pale-blue nightdress was only a few feet away, fluttering over ankles
that were knots of bone in the neck of red pompon
slippers. Mrs Blake had infantile paralysis when she
was a little girl, Margery had told me. I could still hear
Margery crying. My cheek was on the carpet, and
yellow and green colours blurred and spilled into my
vision, as I raised my head. There were large bare feet
with thick humped toes in front of me now, feet that
belonged to pyjamas. A foot swung under my head
and the instep pushed against my cheek. 'Get up,
you're not hurt.'

'Don't, Jim.'

'I'm not going to touch him. I never did touch him,
remember that.'

I lowered my head and twisted over to my stomach,
folding my arms under my forehead, wondering
vaguely whether I should tell the man his feet needed

a good wash. I would have a headache when I woke up in the morning. Perhaps I was getting a touch of summer sickness, from being naked in the hot, spinning boil of the sun like that. I'd stay in bed for a day or two, and Mrs Ranier would come and see me; she might even bring me breakfast in bed. There was something else beside my head worrying me, too; something that had been so frightening I had been afraid of sleeping. If I went to sleep now the pain in my head might be gone when I woke up.

Out of the darkness again, as my face became cool and wet under a gentle touch. 'Thanks,' I whispered. The focus of returning consciousness was sharp, though, and when I looked up at Mrs Blake I knew what had happened, and where I was. She was watching me, with flickering eyes, as she bathed my forehead with a flannel. 'Nothing's wrong,' she said. The water was dribbling down one side of my face and under my collar. 'I'm all right,' I said, 'that's enough.'

The flesh of Mrs Blake's cheeks was swollen and flushed, her eyes were blank under fidgeting lids, her hair a withered tangle pressed flat under a net, and she was frightened. When she jerked her hand from my face she let the flannel drop to my chest. I was on the sofa now.

'Am I all right?' Mrs Blake started to nod her head. 'Yes, you had an accident, that's all – nobody hurt you – a lump on your head is all.' Her head kept jerking up and down as though the movement was involuntary, like the flickering of her eyelids, and her whole body was agitated under her rustling nightgown. I reached out a hand to hold her arm, but she pulled away and wailed, 'Don't you dare touch me,' in the same instant becoming still, the fixity of her attitude such a drastic change in her that I could only stare dumbly into a dazed steadiness of her eyes.

'Where's Mr Blake?'

'He's talking to the doctor.'

'The doctor?'

Her hands plucked at the waist of her dressing-gown and twisted it. 'Don't talk like that, Robert – don't look like that.' She faded from sight. I had been watching her hands as they melted into writhing snakes of light across a blackness. 'I'm all right,' I heard my voice distinctly; there was nothing wrong with my voice.

'It serves you right – it does – after what you have done . . . admit it, Robert, admit it.' She seemed a distance away now.

'Nothing's happened,' I said, making the effort and opening my eyes. Her face was a pink balloon with human features smudged on it. 'Mr Blake's feet smell,' I said. The balloon bobbled up and down, and because I could not be bothered watching, I closed my eyes.

The voice said, 'What's your name?'

Thumbs poked into my eyes. I shook my head violently and pressed the lids up. Long, white hands flicked away to disclose an old man's face behind them. 'I asked you your name,' the old man said.

'I'm Robert Henderson.' The man had the same kind of face as Mr Robbins: yellow and slack with sagging lines.

'Where do you live, Henderson?' The eyes were sagging, too.

'I live in Hobson Street.'

'It's very late for you to be still here – sit up and get ready to go.' The pot-bellied little figure of a man in a black suit went with the face and the voice: he was standing over me now. I sat up to dizziness.

'I'm a doctor, Henderson. You have nothing to worry about.'

'My head's hurting,' I said, and pushed out my hands, wanting the doctor to hold them.

'That girl is hysterical with fright, Henderson. I hope a little pain is not all you're going to suffer for your action.' The doctor's round belly pumped with his words as though it was being brought into use to help his lungs sustain the deep and solemn power of his voice. 'You get no sympathy from me or anyone else.'

'I can't see properly, Doctor . . . I can't. My head hurts.'

'You may have been knocked out, Henderson. You are no doubt mildly concussed. Rest for a couple of days – I've no doubt the police will see you get that – and you'll have no other ill-effects.'

'Margery, tell them to talk to Margery. Where is Margery? Margery will explain.'

'She was lucky her father saved her before you could really hurt her.'

The burn of her cheek against mine, and her panting breath; her body was rising in excitement. Or was it the effort of our contest? Then, later, she had screamed into the light. She had wrenched her head sideways, trying to escape; there was an awful bump, then her cry, and she screamed into the light. It occurred to me out of the blue, or whatever I was in, that I was a sex maniac.

I choked, and dragged myself to my feet, again reaching out to grasp the doctor by the shoulder and lean on him. There was a scuffle about me, a windmill of effort, and the doctor was backing away into the giddy room. 'You can stand on your own two feet,

Henderson. Don't be weak.' Then the shoulder was no longer under my grasp, the room swayed and became still as pain split my head and I stumbled the few steps to the black and solid piano and pressed back up against it.

'I don't feel right.'

'You'll improve slowly. The grogginess will wear off.' The doctor was standing near the door, holding the lapels of his coat in his hands, his head cocked to one side, the ruddy smoothness of his baldness above a domed forehead as old as the sag of the flesh of his face. 'You are better to walk out of this particular trouble on your own feet,' he was saying.

'It wasn't just me.'

Mrs Blake appeared behind the doctor. Her face was still puffed and boneless, without depth of feature. 'A policeman is here,' she said. 'He wants to talk to Margery. Is he all right?' She pointed at me.

'Groggy, that's all.' The doctor patted her back. 'I certainly will not permit Margery to be questioned now,' he said. 'She is under sedation. Don't worry, Mrs Blake, I will speak to him myself. There is no question of that now.' As he went out of the door, he said over his shoulder, 'Your own feet and on your own shoulders, Henderson – if you have any self-respect.'

'What does he mean?' Mrs Blake asked.

'He thinks – he thinks, I don't know . . .' I rubbed my hands under my eyes. 'I'm very sorry, Mrs Blake, for what happened.'

Though my legs were weak, and my head still aching in jolts that felt like the padded blows of a fist, I was getting better. 'How's Margery?' There was something wrong with my voice; it was blurred and weak.

'She's – she's asleep.'

134

'Mr Blake hit me, didn't he? I was sitting on the chair, I remember, and he must have hit me.'

'It served you right. Don't say anything about it, Robert. Don't tell the police anything; Mr Blake has a bad temper, and he'll be sorry in the morning. I don't want my little girl's name in the paper. I couldn't stand it. Please don't say anything to the police. Don't admit anything.'

'I won't say anything about Mr Blake. It must have looked pretty bad to him. But the doctor——'

'He didn't know you were hit that hard, Robert. It's not about Mr Blake hitting you, Robert. It served you right. It's that you must not admit anything to the police, please, Robert. Mr Blake will change his mind in the morning.'

She was speaking in a terrible whisper, her lips parting and snapping shut in extravagant movements, as she held herself rigid, trying to suppress her tremblings. But her nightgown still quivered to the agitation of her narrow shoulders, and her head ticked back and forward on her stiffened neck.

'You must understand,' she was mouthing. 'Don't say anything about what you did to Margery. Don't. Everybody will know it was her. Don't say anything. Mr Blake will change his mind in the morning.' As I rubbed the back of my hands over my eyes, she raised an erratic voice. 'There's a policeman here. Don't you understand? The neighbours heard, and Mr Blake is talking to him now. He's in a terrible temper. I won't have my little girl dragged through the mud. You mustn't say what you did.'

'I didn't do anything, Mrs Blake.' The back of my hand was wet under my nose. 'I don't want to see a policeman. It's not right. Margery will tell you. It was

135

nothing, really.' More words slobbered against my hand, and because my body began to shake, I turned and put my face down against the cool blackness of the top of the piano. When I looked up again this policeman was in the room.

This policeman carried fat like an immense, lop-sided ball below his belt, his pot-belly being balanced by the equal curve of his backside.

'You're the Henderson boy?' he said, wheezing as though the air that delivered his voice was leaking as it crossed his tongue.

'Yes.'

'You know who I am?'

I nodded: it was stupid, this, I thought; they're going to put me in jail.

'I'm Constable Dobbs,' the policeman said, and turned to Mrs Blake. 'I wonder if you would mind making a cup of tea?'

Her hands jumped high in the air, her whole body shuddered. 'Tea?' she exclaimed. She was old and ugly, the puffiness of her face made the awkward focus of her eyes evil.

'If you don't mind. A nice big potful of tea, please.'

Her nightgown fluttered about her ugly ankles as she moved out of the room like a hurrying sleepwalker. Everything about her was ugly.

This policeman muttered, 'Does a woman good to make a cup of tea,' and allowed his head to roll back towards me: his tired eyes glared over the top of the horn rims of glasses that carried a neat binding of black sticking-plaster on their bridge. 'Wipe your nose, for God's sake, my young buckaroo,' he said. 'You look like a terrible mess.' His uniform coat was loose and crumpled about his shoulders and chest, shining and tight over the circular pressure of his stomach, and loose again, almost like a frill, about his thighs. His trousers bagged like plus fours, the cuffs wrapped and held neatly by bicycle clips. He made the chintzy lounge, the whole frilly feminine niceness of it, look like a room in a doll's house.

I fished a handkerchief out of my pocket and buried my face in it, wishing that I would grow giddy again, even collapse on the floor. Then they would help me.

'Snap out of it.' The wheeze was impatient.

I stood away from the piano and pulled the loosened knot of my tie back into place, and ran a hand around the back of my neck, determined not to be weak any more.

'I'd like to go now, if you don't mind,' I said. Waves of heat flushed over the beating hurt of my head, dimming my eyes, blinking them, so in case I had not spoken clearly, I said again, 'I wish to leave immediately.' My eyes cleared as the man's thick lips rolled back in what might have been a smile.

'You do, do you, my glassy-eyed young tom-cat? Well, one thing to start off with – don't get snooty with me, or I'll boot your backside all the way back to the station. And don't shout like that.'

That was silly: I hadn't shouted. 'I'm sorry . . . it might be my ears.'

'Come on down to the kitchen and get this tea. You look as though you need it more than anybody else. Then we'll have a yarn.'

Mr Blake was standing along the passage, in the doorway of Margery's bedroom, the light burning behind him and throwing his giant shadow right up the wall to the ceiling. Margery was asleep, and not caring. I would watch the shadow, and not look at Mr Blake, move up close to the policeman.

'What about some tea in the kitchen, Jim,' this policeman said.

The shadow drifted and raised a terrible arm that was about to strike me down and I threw myself forward, doubling over and crushing between the wall and this policeman. A rough sleeve roughened up the side of my face and a heavy hand twisted the back of my collar, straightening me up, so that I was staring down the passage, at a light. A fear that I was being held for Mr Blake to strike possessed me, making me swing my head about, to avoid the blows. 'Easy boy, no need to do your block,' the policeman said. Now the fear became the final weakness that would not be suppressed, 'I'm going to be sick,' I choked. This hand jerked forward, almost lifting me off my feet, and I was propelled down to the end of the passage, shoved through the bathroom door. 'Better out than in,' said the policeman, holding me over the lavatory. 'A good auction never hurts anybody.' The direction of the voice changed. 'You'd better keep away, Jim.' A hand shook my neck. 'Up with everything; make a job of it.' This hand was an enormous weight. 'The boy and I will have a yarn in the kitchen and then we'll go.' I was swung right around and steered over to the wash-hand basin. 'Clean up, and we'll get this cup of tea.'

'The snivelling brat looks very sorry for himself now, but don't let that take you in. He's putting it all on, making himself sick, trying to crawl out of it.' Mr Blake was a bastard.

'We'll see.'

My head over the basin, forehead rubbing the tap, one hand splashing cold water up to my face; my head dropping right into the basin, wetting the burning side against the splash of the tap, dribbling a cold stream down my neck, the shocks of cold shaking clear my mind, and so the delusive frights fled as I remained doubled over into the porcelain gleam and I became dulled, almost insensate, knowing that the worst must be finished with, and there could be only little hope. When the policeman finally pulled me up and shoved a towel at me, the house was silent, Mr Blake gone. In the passage again, on the way to the kitchen, I looked back: the door of Margery's bedroom was closed.

This policeman slurped tea from his cup, which he kept wrapped in one hand close under his mouth; underneath, about level with his shoulders, he held the saucer, in which he was careful to catch the slight dribble from his chin. His elbows were on the table, and his eyes closed while he drank, and now and then he grunted. He finished two cups, in which he had dissolved mountainous spoonfuls of sugar, before he bothered to take any more notice of me.

'How are the guts?' he asked.

'Better now.'

'You're looking a bit better, too. The girl's father, Blake – he gave you a thumping, didn't he?' I did not answer. He belched and picked up the teapot. It was empty. 'Damn,' he said. I reached to the end of the table where the electric jug stood. 'There's more hot in here,' I said. 'There's a plug on the wall if you want it boiled up again.'

'She's right,' said this policeman, lifting the lid off the teapot. 'Fill her up with what's there. I gather you know your way around this place.'

'I suppose so.'

'You've known the girl a fair while?'

'About a year.'

He emptied the sugar bowl into his refilled cup and stirred it vigorously. 'Jim Blake always did have a temper. We used to play football together in the old days and he'd do his block sometime in a game, never a miss. A bash artist, but a decent bloke. Soon as I saw you, I knew you stopped a few.'

'I'm feeling better now.'

This policeman lifted the cup and saucer to the level of his chin and dropped his head. But he kept his eyes open this time, like a very old dog. 'I'd have had Blake in here, but you seemed so scared stiff of him that I thought better of it. We wouldn't have got anywhere, the mood he's in now, anyway. And his missus is hopeless.' He curled his lips over the edge of his cup, took a huge slurp of tea, sighed and said, 'So you tell me what happened.'

'I can't, that is – I'm not sure.'

'The girl's been bashed, Henderson, and you're responsible, according to Blake. The doctor said she was hysterical, her face cut – could be bad for you.'

'I didn't hurt Margery.'

He finished his tea with a second gulp and banged the cup and saucer on the table. 'You were at it when Blake came upon you. You didn't care what you were doing to her. You were going to bash her into it. You wanted your end in, eh?'

That was it, the filthiest thing of all. 'Don't you talk like that,' I cried, and would have jumped to my feet, full of caring again. But this policeman reached across and slapped a hand on my head. His finger-tips almost lifted my scalp off. 'Hold your horses, Henderson.

There's been enough fuss in this house for one night.' The hand lifted and dropped to the table, beside the cup. 'You've only had half your tea – finish it.' The hand was huge and heavy, with knuckles like so many little fists.

I whispered, 'You shouldn't have spoken like that.'

'Remember what I said about kicking your backside all the way to the station.'

'It's not right to talk like that about decent people. I don't care.' I watched the hand, sure that it would soon clench and be raised against me.

'You'd be surprised about decent people,' he said. 'A couple of months ago I answered a call to a decent man's house. The decent man was roaring drunk. Among other things, the decent man had chased his wife all over the house and piddled on her.' His colourless eyes were hard, glass-dry and huge over his glasses as he growled into my face. 'It's no use looking shocked at me, my young buckaroo. Being decent doesn't impress me in the least.'

'I'm talking about really decent people.'

'It doesn't matter. Being really decent doesn't stop people from doing stinking things. It makes them sorry afterwards, that's all.'

The sludge of porous skin over his flat features was becoming ruddy with irritation. He held his head so low to glare at me that I could see a white excrescence of skin, like a huge wart, on his bald crown. 'Now answer just one question for me,' he was saying slowly, only the slightest growling trace of wheeziness in his voice. 'Did you try to bash the girl into it?'

I tried to speak, to act, but it was no use. The slime was all over me now, and nothing really mattered. I wasn't afraid, either; it was just that nothing mattered.

If anything did, I could not think of it. I must be able to speak, though. It was nothing like that. 'It was nothing like that.' I could speak. I tried to think of Margery and almost succeeded: of how she had sat across the table from me, in this kitchen, the chessboard between us, with only the spasmodic life of the refrigerator to remind us of time, the soft linoleum of the floor, square-patterned and as clean as the cream-painted walls: I tried to think of all the time I had spent with Margery here, arguing and laughing, but could reach only the verge of memory. 'I can't think,' I said.

'Finish your tea, boy, I think you've had plenty for one night.' The policeman's belly bumped the table as he got to his feet. 'I'll have a few words with Blake, and then we'll go.' The big hand did clench, and was raised, but only to touch me on the shoulder. 'Don't worry, son, the world is not ending.'

I listened to the clump of the policeman's feet and wished the world really would end, or that I could run away. The policeman would be telling Mr and Mrs Blake that he had everything in hand; he used to play football with Mr Blake. There was something wrong with me, I knew. The difficulties in recent years caused by riding a bike or being jolted around on a tram or train had not been the natural result of unavoidable agitation, but the very first signs of mania. I opened my eyes wide, quickly, and jerked my head up from my arms, and this policeman was at the kitchen door, watching me.

'I'm a filthy pervert,' I mumbled.

'Yes – I bet you are,' he said. 'But we'll talk about it all in the morning. Everybody's agreed on that, especially Mrs Blake. C'mon, we're going.'

I followed the light of his torch around the back and down the side of the house. My legs were surprisingly steady. A wind had livened in from the west, breaking up the blackness of the sky into black clouds, and finding a vague light between them, so that now the night was grey, and the humped side of Trig Hill directly ahead was discernible. From the lounge window a few cracks of light shone from behind curtains and blinds, furtive and ashamed. The wind was sea-fresh and cleansing, good enough to wash in, and I began to doubt whether anything had really happened to me at all. Then the gate clicked and he held it open for me to go through. The swing of his torch flashed across my eyes, and I winced, knowing full well what had happened. On the footpath outside, balanced against the fence, was a bike.

'I'll double you back to the corner of Hobson Street,' he said. 'You can walk the rest of the way.'

'Aren't you going to take me to the station?' I said.

'What the hell for?' he growled. 'You haven't done a thing as far as I'm concerned. And if you have, I know where to find you.' He hoisted a leg over the saddle of the bike and flashed his torch on the few inches of bar between the periphery of his stomach and the handle bars. 'I don't suppose you can squeeze in there?' he asked.

'No, I don't think so.'

'Damn, we'll have to walk. I'd better see you out of the confounded neighbourhood.'

'It's all right, really. Honestly, I'll go by myself. It's all right.'

'Not in your sweet life.'

We had not gone far when this policeman slapped

the seat of his bike and uttered a noise like the sudden clearance of a blocked drain. 'Hells, bells,' he said. 'Fancy messing around with a daughter of Jim Blake's right on his doorstep. You ought to get a medal.'

7

It was still with me next morning, this idea of Harry
Maddox, with gun, and Robert Henderson, with Mrs
Ranier, coming together over at the Crown land in a
meeting of some intimacy, at least between the gun
and Mrs Ranier. This fact that this idea was still with
me didn't worry me the slightest, for I was without
feeling from the neck up now and, even more than
yesterday, wanted to pay Mrs Ranier back. Whatever
happened, the blame would be mine; I was a sex
maniac anyway. I looked about my bedroom, at the
fireplace long in disuse hiding a whole box of childhood toys behind a heavy brass screen, at my new
cricket bat in the corner, its willow-cleanness freshly
oiled, at the clumsy, disc-shaped book-ends I had made
at primary school, at the dull walls of familiarity that
enclosed me, and at the ceiling, one corner of which
was stained in a curious pattern that a leak in the
roof had produced many years before. This leak didn't
help. Spitting from the sky, seeping through iron,
filtering past wood and lining, water had found a
crack in the plaster and spread, and even after the
roof was mended the brown trails writhed and
thickened before finally drying into a permanent impression of squashed rottenness, with dribbles running
out from it in thin spidery lines, like tendrils of hope
for the spread of evil. This was writing on a ceiling
for me, so I decided that it would be a wise move to
die. I would swim out from Raggleton Beach until I

145

was tired and able to rest for ever; my body would sink into the vast silence of the ocean, tumble about with the tides, the wash and bite of salt water purifying my stained flesh before it was delivered back to the beach for a forgiving burial. Everybody would be dreadfully cut up at the funeral.

The door-knob rattled and my step-mother poked her head into the room. 'I've called once,' she said. 'The trays will be ready soon and you're not up yet.'

'Righto,' I said, sighing very hard.

According to the wardrobe mirror there was only a small lump on my forehead, not bigger than a shilling, and the skin was discoloured only slightly; even my right ear, which had been the centre of a throbbing ache the night before, did not appear swollen, and its slight redness could well have been caused by my sleeping on that side. There was a surface brightness to my eyes that was undoubtedly the result of some demented condition, such as an excess of hormones, and the moist redness of my lips clearly indicated weakness and depravity. I began to feel another hint of my mania and, sure that my lustful nature was threatening to take control, banged my head against the mirror again and again, welcoming the pain that fired from the tenderness of my forehead. When the groaning effort of my action became too much I had to desist, blind and spinning – to realise as the pain lessened that the real cause of my trouble was a prickling fullness of bladder.

And then I thought of Mrs Ranier again, and of what had to be done, and the thought grew with me until my hostility to the opposite sex assumed such proportions that even Miss Rookes sitting up in bed and carefully keeping the covers up to a point just below her chin and chittering happily did not appeal to me. Even when she said, 'It's another new and wonderful day, Robert.'

When he heard his breakfast tray being brought in, old Robbin lurched into a sitting position, his lower eyelids hanging down to expose the scarlet of their inner surface, his dry lips muttering over his gums, his hand fumbling out to a glass of water that contained his teeth, his ample stomach heaving with wind that he expelled with such good breeding that the bowel noise had a sort of Oxford accent, too. He was right: it was that kind of a morning.

The whole house was dry and dull; there wasn't much in anything. I knew what had to be done, and was able to go into Mrs Ranier's room without too much effort, thump her tray down noisily because she didn't stir, pull the window drapes back with a couple of swings and announce, 'I want to talk to you.'

Her eyes were heavy and she did not bother to lift her head. There was nothing but the sharpness of her nose, the smouldering mess of her hair. The room's air was stale and dusty and the disorder of her belongings slatternly. There wasn't any magic left anywhere.

'It's important,' I said. 'I want to talk with you.'

'Go ahead,' she murmured.

'Away from here. I'll meet you at the post office at ten o'clock.' I had everything worked out like that, you see.

'Good heavens,' she said, taking the trouble to open her eyes.

'You've got to,' I said. 'We'll go for a walk.'

'Oh, dear,' she said, a hand up to her neck and pulling a mound of blankets about her ears.

'It's important and you have to come,' I said loudly.

147

She squiggled her head about on the pillow and murmured, 'I really believe I do, too.' She yawned. 'A little fresh air might help everything, I suppose.'

After breakfast I telephoned Harry. He didn't back down, of course. I made sure I was out of the house early. The sky was dubious and though there was a wool-bin scattering of clouds in the only rift of blue to the south there was no real threat of rain. Being a Saturday morning, the town was drowsing. Everybody would be hanging about their quiet houses, unwashed and drinking cups of tea, with no particular plans for the day except those concerning the lawn, the vegetable garden, the pub, and food. I wandered about for a while, and then took a roundabout way to this post office; the deviousness of my route made the journey easier. Not until the last minute, when turning up from the corner, was I making the direct approach, and then it was the bottom-of-the-sea for me: my breath bubbled, my ears blocked under the pressure, my eyes strained into watery air; given sudden relief from this strain, I would have had an acute attack of the bends. This post office was three storeys of ferro-concrete, no ledges, parapets, ornamentations, or anything else to break off on to the heads of passers-by in the event of an earthquake; it looked like a lidless shoe-box, inverted. From the foyer, next to the inland and overseas boxes, I could see the Moderne Hat Shop across the avenue. These hats were the usual concoctions on wooden stands, and no help, because heads appeared in them – women's heads, vaguely like old tennis balls seen down the sights of a gun. I looked above the shop, across the river, to the south plateau hill and the road that wriggled up its side in escape from the valley, and was wondering whether I should try and wriggle out with this road when foot-raps on the pavement became painful clips to my ears, and the road twisted, and was still, the hill shifted and loomed nearer, and when my gaze dropped the women's hats nodded through misty glass, against my face. The sound of the footsteps grew louder, I could not wait, so moved out of the foyer for her to see me: I knew it was her, and that I had to survive in her sight.

She was almost on top of me when she stopped, mouth almighty and eyes wide, exaggerating as usual.

'Robbie – you always manage to startle me.'

'Sorry.'

Despite her fluttering act, she was looking old and tired, and there was no real life in her: her face seemed faintly blotchy, its lines deeper, and the blue of her eyes was white-flecked; her hair rusted and dull, knotted at the back of her head, as coarse as rope, making her neck long and thin. The white beret cocked on her hair, the sloppy green sweater, the donegal skirt and thick brogues were disguising crumby flesh and bone. I didn't like her.

'Where do we go from here?'

'Around the corner, and only about ten minutes to open country and not a bad walk.'

She did not remark on my appearance, so presumably it did not match my feelings – if it had, it would have been a clear subject for comment: eyes bloodshot and rolling, mouth grimacing, that sort of thing.

149

We went along Fitzroy Street, an empty place, where wooden buildings edged the footpath, offering nothing to the passer-by but closed doors and dark windows and the faded nameplates of backyard industry: a street better deserted, where paint flaked, spiders webbed, and weeds choked through the cracks in the asphalt, and echoes were in wait for the slightest sound. From the quay, next street down, the wool-sheds and warehouses showed their scurfy backs, and ahead was the crumpled edge of town, where the way dwindled into metal, and ragged lupin and rush took over the lumpy ground.

'I'm sorry about yesterday,' she said.

'So am I.'

'It's that look you give me, old chap. It has a queer effect on somebody like me, and you started it, after all.'

She was walking very quickly, always the hurrying one, not bothering to look to the right or left, or to me, which was probably just as well.

'After you left me on the beach, I sat down in the water and told myself, "old girl, you're going out of your mind," and that led to all sorts of decisions.'

She said this, and no more for some time, and there didn't seem anything for me to say at all. Then she broke out afresh, this time of her impressions of Mr Robbins, who, she said, was taking every opportunity to engage her in conversation in the obvious hope of one day being able to pinch her in the bottom. She raced this out with growing life, and gave details of what she described as an old dog's snufflings, and it was possible that this was her tangential approach to

the snufflings of a young dog. I couldn't be too interested, being conscious of the inevitability of events
which had this final momentum to carry us where we
had to go, and the going was downhill all the way.
I had great faith in Harry.

She livened up tremendously as we walked; all the
sagginess about her vanished, she became stronger of
voice, and all the old buoyancy restored the lilt of her
body.

'Cheer up, Robbie,' she said, jiggling my elbow.

'I'll try,' I said.

'It's all forgotten between us – and I promise I'll
never worry you again. I *did* worry you, didn't I?'

'It doesn't matter,' I said.

She released my elbow and stretched her arms above
her head, taking a deep breath instead of yawning
though, and her teeth bared and bit on the air, and I
roughed her across her shoulders with my hand, and
said, 'Give you a race to the bridge,' because I had
to do something. She might have been waiting for this,
so promptly did she break into an elbow-flapping,
awkward-gaited run that was a joke, really, as I kept
a yard behind, wanting her to think she might beat
me. At the last moment I ran past her and clattered
on to the footbridge and twisted around to watch as
she stumbled to a breathless halt. She was momentarily
distressed by her effort and leaned against the side of
the bridge, and I was nearly satisfied. This bridge was
just a board-and-rail affair over a ditch at the dead-end
of the road, which lost even the dignity of metal on
the other side of the ditch, and soon was nothing but
a clay track. We stood on this bridge for a few
moments until she fully recovered her breath. She was
happy now, the glint of this mischief in her eyes.

151

'It's so silly,' she said. 'Especially when I've decided to become a sensible married woman again.'

'Eh?' I'm afraid I did say that.

'I'm going to become a sensible married woman again,' she said, turning and leaning on the rail.

'What do you mean?'

'I'm going back to my husband – I've made up my mind.'

'I thought . . . well, you said you were divorced, y'see.' I had to explain my interest, to myself as much as to her.

'The divorce is not final yet, and George wants to call it off, and perhaps he's right. In fact, I'm sure he's right. It's my only hope.'

She was serious, as though this announcement was of great importance to me – as though it explained something. I stamped my feet on the bridge and said, 'Let's go on.' It was too late to worry about these things now.

She took my arm and said, 'Robbie – you don't know what you've done for me.' Her cheeks were clear again, the grip of her hair to the back of her head had loosened and was less severe : except for the lines, and these had almost disappeared, she couldn't have looked much younger had she been my age. 'Don't be so melancholy, young man,' she said. 'I'm not a fool any longer, for the first time in years . . . but I suppose I'm sounding like one to you right now.'

On our way again, we skirted a patch of blackberries in the high banks of the season, brushed through manuka scrub, and then reached a clearing of clay and stones with clumps of rushes that disguised its gradual slope to a dry creek-bed, on the other side of which, behind a fringe of gorse, was the place where the old man had been gathering firewood nearly a year before. Harry would be in the trees near there, waiting.

She stopped and complained that she had scratched her leg on a blackberry vine. She rubbed this leg, bending forward, half-lifting the bare flesh of it, so damned naked in a peculiar way that I wanted to tell her something of great consequence to us both, as an explanation for what was about to happen to her: this something of great consequence was tender, I knew, because my feeling was tender, but what the something actually was I did not know: some truth, the inspiration of my emotion, was there all right, but I could not grasp it. The shape of her back, the hang of her body bending, the intentness with which she stared at her rubbing hand, the very sound of the rub of her flesh all added up, I suppose, yet my answer was not in the addition, otherwise surely it would have been clear. When she looked up our eyes met in an exchange of some feeling that worried her, I could see: perhaps she understood me better than I did myself. When I looked away she kept her eyes on me: I felt her eyes and started walking on, before she learned too much.

'Come on,' I called, hurrying, nearly slipping, in my anxiety to get down the slope, zigzagging to avoid the brown clumps of rushes and scoured hollows, and making a running jump from the bank to the creek-bed, where the smooth scales of silt crackled into powder under my feet. She did not want any more games, though, and came down the slope slowly, no longer the hurrying one. I walked down the dry creek-bed and found the track up the opposite bank and through the gorse, and called to her again, pointing the way. My voice was not exactly right. As soon as she was down, I moved up the track, to the edge of a desolate flat, where the grass was coarse and flax clumps were shredded and yellowing, and small stands of rickety trees clung with exposed roots to shingle and clay. The banks of the dry creeks that ran haphazardly parallel every few hundred yards ahead were marked by a stunted heightening of manuka or gorse. The river was about a mile to the right, behind a curving bush line that spread overland higher upstream, making a true bush of the Crown land; but here, right in front, was the dirt and dandruff stuff.

Mrs Ranier came slowly after me, carefully, and her care was not only for her foothold, or the protection of her legs from gorse scratches.

When she reached my side she said, 'I'm not sure that this is my idea of a walk.'

'There are tracks all over here and the going's easy,' I said. 'It's interesting in a messy way.'

She was looking at me still, and some damned emotion of hers drenched all over me, making me weak: there was softness and hesitancy of puzzled care in her eyes, and not for herself, either: that was what might hurt later.

'You don't have to come if you don't want to,' I said, and turned away from her once again, and walked on, being, naturally, the same old Robert Henderson, boneless and sweating, but in the right place now – where all the rabbits lived. But I was going to get within range of the gun if I had to crawl the rest of the way. This gun had a worn stock with all the marks and discoloration of long handling; underneath, for almost the entire length of the stock, were deep notches we had cut to make it look good; the metal of the barrel was smoky dull and the sighting bead painted white, again for effect. It was there, this gun, a couple of hundred yards away, in the wilting tangle of undergrowth about the huddle of trees with leaves of sickly spikes. Harry was there with it, shadowed and hidden, and she would come near, and it would be fired.

'Come on,' I called to Mrs Ranier, pulling through the tangle of growth on rutted ground, not following the track, desperate for the shortest distance to an ending: for some reason, I was sure we were at an ending. Moving was pushing, as though against a strong wind, with my eyes streaming out of flopped head; but I lasted, and the rotting logs were at my feet, crumbling and soft to kick, and the stand of trees was near, of trees thick and high with deep enough shadows. There was nothing more for me to do now but wait. I could look to her as she followed me again, keeping to a track, neither worried nor angry, blank of any expression I could discern, but having purpose, for she was watching me all the while, like a weasel approaching a rabbit. Her body was brimming in the wavering line of her strong walk, and it seemed that she must have some intent, though there was nothing in her face – nothing where there had always been something. This rabbit wanted to start squealing, as she hesitated, not far from me.

'Cheer up,' she said.

My breath was holding as I waited. There was kindness in her eyes now, and this something again, and only by anger could I save myself from weakness. I turned towards the trees and shouted, 'Harry.' This was the command of my anger, for he had waited too long for what he had to do.

There was a movement in the ragged canopy of leaves and branches, and a brittle crackling as the

155

shadows were made hollow by a flickering twist of colour near their surface. The trees shrivelled into pathetic shapes again, and became inadequate and feeble: it was as clear as the sour sky what had happened. Then Harry stepped out from the trees, the rifle clutched in one hand and held above his head as he trampled through the high undergrowth. He had no guts even for what he'd said he would do.

Clear now, he walked towards us, wide-shouldered, a ridiculous grin on his face. He called, 'Fancy seeing you here, Roberto.' He wasn't so good in his voice though; it was nervy and uncertain. He really wasn't doing so well at all now that he was so near: he was awkward, a loon with a grin that could crack his head in half.

'A friend?' Mrs Ranier was saying.

'Yes,' I said.

'Harry Maddox,' he blurted. He stopped, twisting a heel in the ground with a mumbling laugh. 'I'm out after rabbits.' Then this fool flicked his eyes about and blushed.

There was nothing for me but the feeling of being licked hollow: there was no anger or sorrow at this, either: this losing was something I was used to, and could take without fuss any longer. After a few seconds the hollowness was filled by what I was, really, I suppose, and the fact that there was a point past which Harry could not go did not hurt me, nor did I think less of him: she had beaten me, and now she had beaten him, and that was that for silly boys who talked big. Nothing would ever happen to Mrs Ranier.

'I saw you in there,' I said. 'I thought it was you.'

'Robert is not at all happy this morning, so perhaps you can cheer him up,' Mrs Ranier said.

'Would you like me to come with you and try for a few shots?' Harry said, blurting with nervous laughter again.

'Fine,' I said. 'You come.'

From right beside me, Mrs Ranier said, 'Robbie, you haven't introduced me to Mr Maddox.'

We spent an hour wandering about the flat and, though we saw no rabbits, we fired a few shots at a small tin we perched against a tree. Mrs Ranier did most of the talking and laughing, although Harry thought she was wonderful, and did his share. I was the quiet one, of course. When she was some distance from us, setting up the tin again after I had hit it, Harry said to me, 'She's a great one – there's nothing wrong with her.'

'No,' I said. 'She's really all right, I suppose.'

Harry frowned, and his frown was as big as his silly grin had been big. 'It was just as well you called out and stopped me putting a few shots near her,' he said. 'I was just going to cut loose.'

His was a harmless lie to save face, and I let him get away with it.

'I never really meant you to – I just wanted to see how far you would go,' I said.

My lie was something else again, of course.

3

Even though it was just past noon, and anybody in the house who saw me might think it strange, I went to Mrs Ranier's room. She had asked me to come, and was waiting for me.

'Sit down and let's have this talk,' she said. 'Our

157

positions seem to be reversed from this morning.'

I went across to the easy chair. My face in the mirror-door of the wardrobe was rather pale and bashed under an untidy mop of hair which needed watering into some kind of order.

'I liked your friend Harry,' said Mrs Ranier.

'He's all right,' I mumbled.

'You obviously have something on your mind to look so absolutely shattered – don't think I didn't notice anything this morning. What's wrong? It can't all be that ridiculous business on the beach yesterday.' And then, because I remained silent, she said, 'Don't be a ninny, Robbie.'

I got to my feet slowly. In the past, anger had made me foolish in dealing with her : now I would be careful. 'You've no right to come here, spoiling every-thing——' But it was no use trying to think, so I let myself go : 'Don't you call me names. You've done dirtier things and run away or what are you doing in a place like this?' I paused, and then cried, 'You're an English bitch – there, you're a damned flop.'

She frowned, turned her back on me, and stared out the window, where the rhododendrons and hedge showed now a rust-streaked greenness that was stale and dry, and cobwebs, like the thin lines of age, powdery white to the sun, were slack between the leaves. She straightened and, still keeping her back to me, said, 'You're much too close to the mark. But I suppose I asked for it.'

'It doesn't matter,' I said, and slumped down on the bed, elbows on knees, cheeks in cupped hands. 'It's just that when I was getting a grip on the way things are, my whole life gets messed up.'

'It's not really, Robbie.'

158

I looked up and saw that she had turned around. Her face was shadowed and grave under the glow of her hair and she was only sad, and not angry.

'You don't know the whole story,' I said. 'Mr Blake gave me a hiding last night.'

'I beg your pardon?'

'He hit me.'

'What on earth for?'

'He caught Margery and I – y'know, kissing and things.'

'Robbie, darling——' and suddenly she was actually smiling, '—you glorious idiot.' Then, as though she realised how desperate it all was, she assumed a solemn face. 'I'm really very sorry, of course.' Her eyes opened wide and she brought the long fingers of her hands to her cheeks.

'You're overdoing it,' I snapped into the false sympathy of her gaze.

'Tell me about it,' she said and, somewhat to my own surprise, I found myself doing just that.

She asked only one question after I finished my story: 'What did the policeman think about it all?'

'He thought it was a joke.'

'There – I can't see a tragedy of great magnitude here, old chap.' She was scarcely more than a silhouette against the window; her voice was quiet and even, without a hint of feeling. This was just a small problem it seemed. 'From what I understand, it's just another case of a quick-tempered father coming across his daughter at the wrong time.'

'I did not expect you to be sorry,' I said.

'Not so bitter, please. You made love to a girl, got caught by her father, and survived after a lot of fuss. Nothing better could happen to you. That's a part of

159

becoming a man – getting into trouble over girls. You're the better for it.' She was quite emphatic.

'That's hard to believe, honestly it is.'

'Always make an adventure of women, Robbie, and you'll never have the slightest difficulty with them. Occasionally they'll cry and fuss, but they'll love it, believe me. The storm last night was an adventure and everybody involved will think of you with much more respect.'

'Eh?'

'And if the news gets around, every girl in town will think you're a Don Juan, and the boys will be jealous of your experience.' She hesitated and spoke more slowly. 'Even I see you in a different light.'

I rubbed my hand around a neck stiff with worry, blinking at her. 'You do?'

'It means that you know that much more about life.'

'There's something,' I burst out. 'The policeman did say I deserved a medal. There's something that indicates you jolly well might be right.'

She looked at me quite sadly again. 'My final advice, old man, is that you should go around to Margery's this afternoon and settle everything. I'd like to think that you had a grip of . . . of the way things are, before I leave.'

'Leave?'

'Yes. I made a long-distance call to my husband last night and told him I would try again.' Her lips flicked about in a weak smile. 'He was delighted even to know where I was. So I'm going to become a suburban housewife again.'

'Lots of things have been happening to us,' I said, getting up from the chair, wanting to be away from her, even though – or was it because? – she had become so much less hateful now. 'I hope you've got a grip on things, too.'

She moved away from the window. 'No doubts,' she said. 'Despite everything, before my wobbling becomes disastrous, I'm going back. By the time I'm middle-aged I'll have sons almost as old as you.'

'I suppose it's all right,' I said.

'I suppose so, too,' she said, in a sharp, queer voice, and damn me if her face wasn't quivering, and even more out of whack than usual.

'Hey,' I said. 'You're going off the deep end.' Both my hands raised of their own accord, it seemed and on strange impulse I lifted them higher and, moving forward, took her by the shoulders. 'You're as bad as I was a minute ago,' I said. She moved right against me; her face rubbed my neck and the side of my jaw for a dazing instant. Her voice gasped, a warm breath against my ear, 'Probably the only thing they will do is play football, Robbie.'

'Who?. . . what's that?'

'My sons — won't that be fine?' Then she was laugh-ing quite strangely and she pushed me away from her and clapped her hands, and was truly not old at all.

'We're friends, good friends after all,' she cried.

'You bet,' I said, and this bad feeling or hate or what-ever it was, had ended. Now we were both laughing in this ridiculous way, and everything had changed, as naturally and as quickly as the taking of a breath. I had to laugh with her, and it was as though I had been swollen with laughter, so long and loud did it come, each guffaw relieving an immense pressure in-side me that I had not known was there until I laughed. She stopped first and then stood with legs apart and hands behind her back, her chest arched

F 161

and full of breath. 'Hey there – look at me,' she growled. 'It's only me.' I understood, and imitated her in turn, plucking my hands at my chest and then tossing them into the air, with a jerking twist of my whole body, hula-style. Then I started to hiccup and had to stop and bend over, dizzy, while she took my shoulders and butted herself gently against the top of my head. 'Out you go,' she said, 'or the whole house will be wondering what on earth is happening.'

I straightened and sidled to the floor, managing to say, 'I'll see you tomorrow.'

But our next meeting was going to be a little sooner than that.

8

By two o'clock I was on my way over to Margery's place, prickling, perspiring, hurrying while my going was good, fear partly anaesthetised by dreams of courage (e.g., if Mr Blake turned nasty and became violent I would drive a hard right to the man's chin in an effort to startle some sense into him. 'And now, Mr Blake,' I would say, 'we will settle this in a more civilised fashion'). I was wearing my best greys, a blue sportscoat and a white shirt with a high collar that made me look rather like a choir boy. I was being fairly calculating, and before leaving home had practised twisting my brown eyes up until they vaguely resembled knots of wood, this to disguise their annoying softness should I have to stare down Mr Blake. After a bad start, this day had turned out in the afternoon pretty much like the day before : the sun a centre of boiling blue, the air simmering into ripples of heat above the surface of the streets. A few lawnmowers chuffed, a few kids called out to play; these were the only sounds of life. Down at the beach, though, the dunes would be covered with hot people and the surf full of splashing bodies. As I pressed on, my courage weakened, and I had to sustain myself by forcing my mind to another subject, football : the ball was high, the forwards were on top of me, I must go up, both feet off the ground, and give a hunching twist as I take the ball and they hit me; their centre was through and the wing coming up outside him for the pass, and I must try and make him give the pass too soon and get the wing from behind; the scrum was on our goal-line, but we have the ball, the half-back is slinging it back to me as their break-way comes charging down, so I must step outside him and left foot it hard for the line; the same again, on the other side of the field, so I must kick with my right foot now; the ball was on the ground, dribbled ahead by their forwards, no chance of clearing now, so I must dive on the ball and turn my back against their feet; we were only twenty yards out from their goal-line, the half-back signalled, so I must run up on the blind-side, inside my wing, for the ball in my hands and hope of a channel.

But walking down the Blake's path, the gate latched behind me, I began to feel really afraid and, no anaesthetic left, tried to justify this great fear by reminding myself that Mr Blake would soon be assault-ing me. My legs trembled and I hitched my trousers up, unbuttoned and rebuttoned my sportscoat, all the while trying to stop the rot from going too far. My legs were almost melted now, and it was no longer possible to run away; it would even be difficult to walk away; no alternative offered to my standing still and melting away. The creosote wall of the house was firm under my hand, but the feel of the sun and its heat was gone; the concrete path, the border-garden, the backyard hedge and the circular clothes-line behind, all there a second ago, had faded – but I could breath, though. 'Left, right – left, right.' I could speak, too. 'Left, right – left, right,' I repeated, pulling away from the wall, jiggling my shoulders up and down, thumping my arms against my sides, jerking my knees up – and I was actually moving forward, 'hup, one, two – hup, one two,' down the side of the house, eyes closed, and beside the drill numbers of Sergeant Henderson, of the high school cadets, in my mind was, 'You're no coward.'

Constable Dobbs stood at the bottom of the steps leading to the back door, the coat of his blue serge suit over one arm, all the buttons of his waistcoat and the top one of his fly undone, the knot of his red tie pulled out of the grip of his collar-wings; his right hand propped on the curve of his rump and his stomach bulged as though the pendulum of his weight had been swung forward by the pressure it was exerting.

'I'll be damned,' he said.

The back door kicked open with a bang and Mr Blake emerged carrying a cup of tea in each hand. He was wearing old trousers and a grey shirt, the open neck of which bristled with brown hairs. At the sight of me he slopped tea over into the saucers, which in turn dribbled it down his clothes. His unshaven jaw moved up and down as though he was having great difficulty in opening his mouth. In another second, I thought, he'll come tearing down the steps like a madman.

'Mr Dobbs,' I said, with plenty of mute appeal to back up my words.

'No need to panic,' said the policeman, throwing his suit coat over his shoulder.

'It's not that,' I said.

'Of course not, boy,' he said, stamping a foot on the bottom step. 'You seem to have made a good recovery from last night.' He moved up the steps and put out his large hands. 'I'll take the tea, Jim,' he said. 'In another minute you'll be spilling the lot.'

'Mmm?' grunted Mr Blake. He looked like a dazed orang-utang.

'The tea – I'll take my cup.'

Mr Blake took his eyes off me and said vaguely, 'Take it, Ned.'

'Perhaps the boy would like a cup.'

Mr Blake's eyes jumped back to me. 'Would you?' he said.

I tried hard, but could neither think nor feel for the moment, and my only response was a stuttering sound that had to be cut off before it sounded too stupid.

'Do you want a cup of tea?'

'No . . . no thanks.'

Constable Dobbs turned and sat down on a step, emitting a huffing groan as he did so, while Mr Blake shuffled about uncertainly on the top of the landing, now regarding me with a quick glance, now eyeing the policeman. This hair on his chest looked like the bristles of a virile hedgehog.

'How long are you going to stay like that, my young buckaroo?' asked Constable Dobbs, posing his cup and saucer under his chin.

'I'm glad you're in good shape,' said Mr Blake, and his concrete face wavered as though subjected to some internal stress, and then loosened about his teeth in a sudden gap which was a kind of a smile.

'I'm fine,' I managed.

Again Mr Blake was jarred by some earthquake of his emotions, and again the gap opened about his teeth: I half-expected to hear a rumble, for the up-heaval of the serious mass that was his face would have required something around force six on his mercalli scale.

166

'Too bad about last night,' he muttered with this second smile. 'Sorry about it all.'

'I'm awfully sorry, too,' I said, convinced at last that he was harmless. His face reset into unaggressiveness and he sat down on the top step, a natural foundation for the burdensome weight of his body. This hair on his chest now looked more like thistledown that would blow away in the next breeze.

Constable Dobbs slurped a mouthful of tea and grinned. 'Don't look so clueless, boy. The whole schmozzle is over – the girl's got everything back on the rails.'

'You'd better go in and see her – that's what you're here for.' This was Mr Blake, and he actually was rumbling.

I nodded, quite speechless: now it was men I couldn't understand.

Constable Dobbs pushed a thick forefinger up the bridge of his nose to settle his glasses into place, and his right eye puckered up in a rather inexpert wink. 'In you go, son,' he said. For the first time his voice carried a trace of the previous night's wheeziness.

It was incredible that the touch of my legs against the massiveness of their sitting bodies was not a violent contact on my way up the steps. Giddy with puzzled relief, I stepped out of the sun's brightness into the shadowy kitchen that was cool, and leaned against the door behind me, scarcely able to see at first. But I could see Margery. She was statue-still, near the window which opened over the backyard, holding her head to one side as though she was still listening to what was being said outside. Black hair glossing back behind her ears, the oval delicacy of her face flushed, a thick piece of sticking plaster like a crude graft of flesh on her right cheekbone, her eyes deep in stained sockets, she looked as though she had never smiled in her life, and did not expect to. There were dirty dishes on the sink, a frying pan deep with congealed fat on the cold stove; a teapot, an unwashed cup, and a couple of pieces of burnt toast perched on the edge of the table, away from a pool of spilt milk partly sopped up by a dishcloth resting in the middle of it; on top of the refrigerator, in conspicuous insignificance, was an open aspirin bottle.

'Hello,' I said to Margery.

'I'm glad you're well,' she said, in a voice that gave nothing away at all. Then she moved past me as though she was balancing a book on her head. In the living room she swept a newspaper from the seat of one of those metal twists of chairs, and dropped into it, one leg tucked under her bottom as though she couldn't care less. She patted her tartan skirt down over the doubled-up leg that stuck out and I wished she would not sit like that, or wear that black sweater, today of all days: she was getting quite prominent up there in her own way.

'I'm sorry about last night and the trouble,' I said, warming to her nevertheless; no matter how untidy she was, or how awkwardly she sat in chairs, she was my girl.

'It's over and done with now,' she said.

'What's happened, Margery?' I burst out. 'Your father is so – so – tell me, what's happened? I thought it was going to be a terrible fix, and I find it's all over. What happened?'

She wriggled back in the chair. 'Nothing's happened. It's just that everybody had——' she shrugged her

168

shoulders '—Let's not talk about it; it was so silly, after all.'

Silly. I pushed an arm up the frame of the door. 'What on earth are you talking about?'

'It doesn't matter.'

'Something must have happened.'

'Honestly, it doesn't matter.'

'It does matter – or at least I think it does. Can't you say anything else but that it doesn't matter?' My voice did not rise, exactly, but the words gushed out, and at least she stopped wriggling.

'I'm – I'm sorry,' she said. 'It's nothing, really, so I suppose that's why I say it doesn't matter.' She pressed the palms of her hands hard on her ungainly knee and tilted her head, almost snooty about it all. 'I suppose the best way to explain it is to say that Mummy and Daddy and I had a talk, and that I explained everything.'

'That must have been some explanation – what did you say?'

'Oh . . . nothing, really.'

'There you go again.'

A certain concentration of feeling appeared in her steady eyes : she was getting ready to come out of her shell, that was obvious.

'We didn't do anything, you and I,' she whispered. Then a deep breath pushed her body up and she brushed her hand across the top of her sweater, and said, 'Except that you fiddled around here.'

The instant smear of heat on my face seemed to spread down my whole body, and though I dropped my head quickly and rubbed my eyes with a thumb and a forefinger, it was impossible to hide my embarrassment. As my eyes were closed to the rubbing, I heard her say, 'It was as much my fault.'

169

'You must have worked a miracle in making your father change like that,' I finally said. 'He was quite nice to me.'

'I lost my temper, that was all. I saw the whole situation and how beastly they were being to me, so I rushed down to the kitchen after lunch and told them off, really I did.'

'Did you – honestly?'

Obviously she had, though: the vehement tone, the indignant tilt of her head, the flush of her whole countenance were testimony to her words; the flush was the after-glow of an earlier blaze, now showing some signs of rekindling.

'Daddy caved in completely, and Mummy went back to bed with a headache.'

'What exactly did you say though?'

She paused, and again there was an awful sense of embarrassment between us, only this time it was she who was feeling it most. The steadiness of her gaze wavered away and she seemed lost in flustered thought – so lost that she did not bother to hide her discomposure. 'I didn't say much,' she finally said, and then hurried on: 'I want you to know I think it is wonderful of you to come over to try and help me, especially considering that you have a retiring nature. Are you physically and mentally recovered, completely?'

'Of course – it was nothing much, y'know, the whole thing. Your father only knocked me out twice.'

'Yes, I do believe you might have been unconscious for a few seconds – or at least dazed.'

'A few seconds: about half-an-hour, y'mean.'

'Don't be silly. You actually started to walk down the passage and into the lounge once we were inside.'

'I don't remember.' I was wondering why I was not annoyed at her having said I had a retiring nature.

'And I was in fits of tears,' she said.

'Yes, you were.' After a few days, when the dust had settled down, I'd have it out with her: I might be considerate, but I was not retiring; she had a damned cheek to say that after all I'd gone through for her; she'd almost suggested I was timid.

'I can't tell you how sorry I am for what happened to you,' she was saying. She was not quite the Margery I knew: there was definitely something there in her now that was different.

'It was nothing,' I told her. 'I was upset last night – groggy – but today I saw things in their right perspective so I decided to come over here to settle things properly . . . in an adult, civilised way.'

That wasn't bad, I thought; I'd even managed to put a rather superior edge to my voice.

Margery twisted her leg from underneath her and sat almost bolt upright, her cheeks really afire this time. 'You've started kissing me,' she declared. 'You mustn't.'

'Eh?'

'Otherwise I can't – I won't – anyway, it's got to stop.'

I stopped leaning on the door frame and held myself erect, determined to stand up to her, in all ways. 'What a thing to say,' I said, trying hard to think of an insult of my own.

'It's just that it makes everything so wrong,' she said. 'We shouldn't do it – we aren't the kissing type and I'm——'

'Not the kissing type,' I cried. 'What are you talking about?'

171

'This is awful for me,' she was saying. 'I don't want to hurt your feelings.'

I waved a hand towards her and mumbled, 'It's nothing.'

'We'd better get it over with, Robert, otherwise it will be hanging over our heads,' she galloped on. 'We've got to talk about it – you've been kissing me practically every chance you've had for weeks now.'

I was screwing my shoulder against the doorway, trying to hold on from second to second.

'I – I don't mind, really, but the fact is perhaps – at least, I'm *certain* we shouldn't.'

'You mean you didn't like it?' I didn't care that my shock must be apparent.

'All the time I was thinking we shouldn't, perhaps, so I suppose that means that I didn't really like it.'

'Oh.'

'I was worried about telling you, about your pride and how hard it is to explain. But I have to now. Last night – last night – well, it was the straw that broke the camel's back, and I have to explain.'

She was trying to be casual, I knew: she wanted me to be casual, too. 'The straw that broke——' I realised that I was mumbling and shifted to the side a little, so that my back would have better support. 'This is an awful kick in the guts,' I said.

'I'm sorry.' Her face softened. She went on, 'I had to say something as our relationship is intellectual, I think, and we have to be more like brother and sister in some ways as I've told Mummy and Daddy that.' Her sprinting tongue tossed this off in one burst.

'You told——'

'Don't be angry.'

'Stop it,' I said. 'I don't want to hear you talking

about it all like . . . like, well, I simply don't know what.' I plucked at my neck with the same thumb and forefinger I'd used on my eyes a little earlier. 'Brother and sister, eh?'

The look on my face must have been bad, for she unknotted herself and jumped up from the chair, and stood close to me, mussed up but pretty, and said, 'Don't you see it's hard for a girl?' She wanted me to understand some damned thing.

'If it's harder than being a boy it must be awful,' I said.

But after that we were models of self-control and took a chess-board and a couple of glasses of orange-ade outside and sat in the shadow of the garage to play a game. We played this game badly, but I think we both knew that we were only making a demonstration of some sort.

'Would you like to come around tomorrow night after tea?' she asked as I left.

'Thanks,' I said, and then did my best with a bit of a joke. 'That'll be fine – sister.'

2

Mrs Ranier was not in her room when I got back home this late afternoon, so I had to wait. I told my step-mother I was not feeling too well and would not want a meal and then went to bed to sleep with heated restlessness, distressed by strange images that floated about the vaguest of dreams like visual echoes of dirty words. It was about seven o'clock when I awoke, and a shower made little difference to my dullness. I spent some time messing around with my hair, and then brushed my teeth. There was hardly a sign of the lump on my head. I couldn't help thinking about Margery, so I plucked the photographs of her out of the corners of my dressing-table mirror and dropped them behind the fire-screen, into that box of those childhood toys. Another photograph, on the mantelpiece above the old fireplace, of my grandfather, white-headed and proud, standing at the gate with his father, a very old man who had both hands clasping the top of a walking-stick close to the pit of his stomach, created in me a sense of loneliness in this house with the ancestral ghosts, all three generations of them. My great-grandfather's stick was thick and his legs were narrow, so he looked as though he was balancing his old body on a tripod. But there was no doubt about my grandfather: he could stand on his own two legs and throw out the massive chest and stomach of a coachline operator and stock and station agency director. This house must have been fairly new then, but it looked exactly the same as it was now: a few coats of paint, a re-roofing, perhaps, was about all that had been done since. An old house breathes when you are alone in it, especially an elaborate structure of aged heart timber under a fantasy of corrugated iron: this evening I sensed movement in the stuffy air, the sound of floorboards creaking under forgotten feet, the echoes of hearty voices, and it came to me as I stared at this photograph that I was really the only one in the world who was not a stranger in this house. I was awash with the idea of a people who came to a valley, made a little comfortable good, and let it go at that. I couldn't think what I was supposed to make, unless it was a mess.

I wandered around town just before dark, past the cow-country prosperity of the old wooden buildings and the more solid expression of it in the few reinforced concrete places built just before the war. Tony's milk-bar was open, of course, but everything else was shut up, and only a few people drifted about the avenue. I ended up in Custom Quay and walked past the warehouses and river wharf south of the bridge. There was soot in the quiet air and the huge raddled sheds were far too empty and lonely, so I turned towards the western fringe of the town, where the streets were tar-sealed to their grass verges and the bungalows in quarter-acre sections bare of any trees kept their blinds half-drawn. Some of the homes hinted at opulence, with their two storeys, tiled roofs, smooth concrete driveways, large sections of neat lawns and shrubs, room enough for a garden party, perhaps; we had our share of stiff-faced old biddies with a lot of side, and butter-gutted men who smoked cigars.

A pig-tailed little girl was playing hopscotch by herself on the footpath in Sydney Avenue. She was whistling as she balanced on one foot and wriggled her hips to get into position to kick a wooden block. As I reached her, she hopped forward.

'You missed,' I said, seeing the block rest on the chalk-line of the boundary of the square. She looked up. 'It's not as easy as it looks,' she said. 'Now I've got to go back and start all over again.' Her eyes were very clean.

'I bet you don't get far.'

She rubbed her hands down her grubby cotton dress, a skinny squib of a girl, and grinned. 'Want to bet a million pounds?'

'If you like.'

'Righto.' She put her cheeky-little-devil face to one side and added, 'You're too young to be a horrible man, aren't you?'

'I suppose so.'

'That's what I thought,' she said, and lifted the front of her dress and tucked it under the top of white bloomers. 'When I bend my knee to kick my foot, my dress gets in the way and I can't see the block. That's what went wrong last time.'

A middle-aged woman was staring at me from the doorway of a house across the street. She was wiping her hands on an apron.

'I hope you win,' I told the girl, and walked away.

Back home I knocked on Mrs Ranier's door, and because there was no reply, filled with alarm that she might have left at the behest of her husband, who could have raced down from Auckland in a car, and even now be on his way back with her. I threw open her door and found the room cool, with the dead brown wallpaper and the grey dust on the cold shine of the table and mirrors making it as dull as it was cool, as though all that had been so palpable there had fled. The bed was white and smooth, cold, and for an instant I was sure she was gone. Then I saw the hand-mirror and hairbrush and the array of little boxes and bottles on the dresser.

It was ten o'clock when Mrs Ranier came home and the click-clicking of her high heels down the passage did not worry me. Soon after I heard her running a bath. She did not take long, and when she was back in her own room I went to the bathroom myself, wiped the steam off the mirror with the sleeve of my dressing-gown, fixed my hair with a wet comb and cleaned my

176

teeth for the third time that day. Out in the passage, cold after the hot and scented air of the bathroom, I began to shiver as I moved in the quiet darkness, guided by the yellow slit of light under her door. Both Miss Rookes and Mr Robbins had their lights out, so there was no real danger as long as my bare feet were quiet enough; my step-mother slept at the top of the house, off the top passage and past the kitchen, well out of harm's way. I knocked once, opened the door and entered Mrs Ranier's room, neither looking for her, nor thinking of her, because of the importance just to hear this door shut behind me, against the whole world. There was nothing in the world now to stop me from doing what had to be done, now that I knew what it was: there were probably quite a number of times like this in life, when the inevitable was created by the recognition of it, and if you did not recognize it the going from then on would be just too bad, and you'd never quite know why.

'I've come to talk to you,' I said to Mrs Ranier.

She was sitting up in bed, a magazine on her knees, a long-handled hairbrush in her hand, quite surprised apparently. She had been brushing her hair as she read: scarlet sheens of it were smooth down to her shoulders. The bedside lamp was tilted, flushing a hard light against one side of her face and body, accentuating the twist of her features so much that for a moment she really did seem ugly, with nose and chin hooking towards each other in witch profile, her skin so transparent; her whole attitude now was crouched and watchful, and her shadow sprawled obliquely up the wall and became a misshapen blackness on the ceiling.

'Surprised?' I said, moving across the room.

'Yes . . . a little.' She was peering at me, the brush

177

still poised, level with her eyes, peering intently, as though she was hidden, and I was unaware of her scrutiny.

'Where were you today?'

'With friends – they took me out for the day.'

The silk of her yellow pyjama top, loose and sleeveless, flopped across the tremulous flesh quite modestly, but her bare arms and shoulders gleamed, and the slight hang of the silk below the hollow shadows at the base of her neck was no help, either. But I could do what I had to do; there was no need to be afraid of her.

She dropped the brush on the bed and flipped the magazine forward from her knees to her neck, and said, 'What brings you here – no more problems, I hope?' She was being very careful.

'No, everything's fine, honestly. As you said it would be, the business with Mr Blake has blown over, and everything is the same as ever it was.'

'I'm so pleased – but tell me all about it in the morning.'

'I feel like talking to you now. There's not much time.' I hesitated, and added, 'I didn't know you had friends here.'

'Friends of Mr Ranier's. He rang them and they did the right thing, out of courtesy.'

'I see.'

'Do you think you should be in my room at this time of night? What would anybody say?'

'They're all in bed now.'

She sat right up, almost on her pillow, her back against the head of the bed, her knees drawn up high, the blankets barely reaching her waist, and her arms held the magazine under her chin, almost as though

178

she wanted to cover her chest. But she was getting more like the mischievous person of our friendly times together; the lamp's light was a fire-glow on her skin as I got closer, erasing her wrinkles, finding depths in her eyes, and the glisten of moisture on her lips. All the distortion of a moment ago was forgotten; the old witch was no more.

She smiled at me at last. 'Look old chap, unless it is desperately important, I don't much feel like chatting now. Do you mind waiting till the morning?'

'It's important, all right.'

'Oh.'

I had to grin at her pretence of surprise; she was teasing me, I was certain of that.

'All right – we'll talk then,' she said. 'But only for a little while.'

I moved down the side of the bed, not waiting to be asked, and looking at her quite openly; she was full and soft, and so warm that it seemed that the heat was simmering from under her skin; I could feel her warmth as I sat on the edge of the bed, level with her knees.

'What are you holding your book like that for?' I asked.

She shrugged her shoulders. 'I'm reading it,' she said, and frowned. 'Is everything really all right, Robbie?'

'Of course it is.'

'What's so . . . so . . . urgent?' But no matter how cool her eyes tried to be, she was warm.

'I am, Mrs Ranier, I suppose.' I placed my hands on my knees and, twisting slightly, turned more towards her and squared my shoulders to their full width, keeping my chest out, too : it was important to look like a man.

179

'I can't begin to tell you how glad I am that everything is right,' she said, not having the faintest idea what was happening to me; there were secret ways of being a man, too. Her frown had gone, but she was serious. 'A crisis is good for one, I think, especially if you've faced it squarely.'

'You're not a sister to me,' I said, 'I'm sure of that.' It would be a shock to her if she knew what was happening to me just now; why I was so sure.

'I beg your pardon?'

'All this time, I've been stupid, not seeing what could happen for the best, but I know now, and it's all right, so don't worry.'

'What on earth are you talking about?' she exclaimed, and I grinned again at her pretence of bafflement. She changed her tactics immediately. 'All right, old chap,' she said, as though she was speaking to a little boy, 'get it off your chest.'

'I know women now, that's what you've got to realise,' I said, wanting to warn her. 'It's a struggle, isn't it? Not the usual kind of struggle, I suppose, but one in which each side . . . oh, I don't know, really. But if I can't put it into words, I know all about it.'

'That's a little murky.'

I saw that she was amused by my stumbling tongue, and said, 'I want to look at you and touch you,' not giving a damn how amused she was. 'I'm going to do it now.'

'This is no time for jokes, Robbie.' She was rubbing her chin on the edge of the magazine, still pretending.

'You've got to show me, y'see.'

'What?'

'About women – yourself . . . y'know. You've got to,' I said and, sure she would tease me indefinitely, reached out and put my right hand against the base of her neck.

'Stop it,' she said, feigning surprise, twisting and bumping my hand away with her upper arm.

'C'mon,' I said. 'I want to know.' I thrust my hand under the fold of her arms and was groping for the full depth of her softness, when she grabbed my wrist. 'Stop it at once.' Her voice was high: she was slapping it on thick.

'Don't panic,' I said, pulling my hand away.

Even though I was certain she was acting, it was hard not to believe in her dismay: the lines about her eyes and mouth twitched and deepened, and her shoulders hunched, and she brushed her hands up her face, splitting her hair across the sides of her head.

'Robbie, what on earth has come over you?'

I grinned, to make sure she knew that I was not fooled.

'Y'know, Mrs Ranier – I want to, well, y'know . . .'

'I don't know.'

'About women – how it is. I want to know.'

'Oh.' She gave a ridiculous smile, of clenched teeth between stiff lips.

'I know you'll show me,' I said. 'You have to.'

Her eyes hooded, and even as I prepared for some kind of trick from her, she asked, 'Exactly what did happen over at Margery's place?'

'I told you,' I was able to say, even though she had guessed so much. 'Nothing much was said at all.'

'So everything was fine?'

'Yes, Margery had it all straightened out, and Mr and Mrs Blake were very friendly. So was Margery.' I could lie, no matter what she guessed: she could not make me admit anything. 'It was amazing, really, how easy everything was.' I did my best to laugh. 'Anyway, Mrs Ranier, you've changed the subject.'

'I suppose I have.' She lifted her head, deepening the shadowy hollows of her neck, and then fisted her hands up under her chin. 'I could have been terribly angry with you just now, and sent you scuttling from the room. Remember that, young man. And don't be bad-mannered again.'

'Eh?'

'You must not be bad-mannered.'

'Well, I like that – I'm just the same as I ever was. It's always been our understanding that I could . . . learn from you.' I couldn't help raising my voice a little. 'It's always been all right, even though I took fright before. Well, I'm not frightened now.'

'I never suggested that you were frightened.'

'Well, it was there. I mean you saw it.'

She leaned forward, and put a tingling hand against the side of my face. 'Robbie, you and I are allies – we must be careful not to hurt each other.'

'I don't want to hurt you.'

'I know that, but I might feel hurt, nevertheless.'

I said, 'Stop teasing. I'm nobody and I've done nothing and I know nothing, but I'm going to, though, and you're not going to talk or laugh me out of it. You've got to show me, that's all.' I raised both hands and would have grasped her, but she took my hands in her hands and said, 'You're being silly, old chap,' and all I could do was shake my head.

'Robbie,' she shook me by the shoulders. 'Listen to me!'

'No, I won't,' I said, and grinned. 'You're tricking me again.' The strange thing was, I could not stop grinning: the corners of my mouth felt strained as they dug up the sides of my face. I raised my hand and pressed my cheeks. 'I'm all right,' I said. 'There's nothing wrong with me.'

'Of course there's not,' she leaned away from me against the top of the bed, folding her arms again over the magazine, still using it as a kind of a shield. 'And, Mr Robert Henderson, you are certainly not a nobody, as you described yourself. You're a wonderful person – I've told you that.' Her smile moistened her eyes and softened the sharp bone-lines of her cheeks and blunted her nose. 'We like each other tremendously,' she said, 'don't we?'

'Yes.'

'Then you really don't want to make some kind of a convenience of me, do you?' she said.

Because I had nothing much to lose, I said, 'What you really mean is that – that you've discovered that I'm not the type to . . . well, that there is something wrong with me.'

She shook her head. 'Get that idea out of your mind. It's me there was something wrong with. And if I permit myself to go wrong again, I'm sunk, Robbie, absolutely sunk. I know it, just know it.'

'What about me?'

'You're so right as you are,' she said. 'And I can't afford to take even one more risk.'

'No,' I said. 'Everything is wrong with me now, I feel it: I'm different . . . I don't know why, but I had hopes of you. The things of your body were mixed up in it, but there was something else, too, I don't know what.'

'For heaven's sake, old chap. Don't be so – so downcast.' Her voice was irritable, and she kicked her feet against the blankets as she spoke. 'Remember, you don't know a great deal about me.'

183

I pressed my arms around my chest; my right hand was over the bumping of my heart. 'You're no different from her, or any other women; you're all the same, aren't you?' I said. 'I look at people and I talk to them, and I try to do my very best towards them, but if they're women they might be laughing at me.'

'Look, old man,' she said, as weak as she had ever been, 'your quarrel is not with me.'

'It doesn't matter,' I said. 'You and Margery are just the same.'

'I don't see——'

'She doesn't want me, either. You know it, too.'

She actually winced. 'No, I didn't know that,' she whispered.

'You know, all right. You guessed. There's something wrong with me – that's what you both think.' I rubbed my fist hard against my knee as she became dim to my sight, far away from me. 'The only reason I've thought there was something wrong with me was because of you, but there's not, and I'm going to show you.'

She was talking, even as I pushed my fist out. She was talking, but I would not hear her. I unclenched my fist against some part of her and was tugging the magazine away, anger a hard throb of my mind that blurred sight and deadened sound. The magazine fell from my hand as I spread my fingers and pushed my hand against her; she was the one I could show.

And then, as if my touch was extinguishing it, the warmth of her body cooled. The spasm of my rage passed, leaving me looking at her, hearing her. 'Robbie, it's no use . . . you must leave me alone,' she said. Her shoulders had slackened and her hands were lifeless against the base of her neck, and her face was strangely vacant, as though her spirit, like her warmth, had fled. I pushed my hand between the flesh of her upper arm and her body, roughing her, wanting her anger; but she was pulpy, and without tension or life. Her eyes had lost their sight, but not in anger, as mine had: she was looking into my face, but her gaze was inward, blind to me, and the idea that she could ignore me so completely was shocking.

'It's me against you,' I said, feeling the first weakness of fear. 'I'll show you.' My left hand was against her too as I stood up. 'You can't fool me again.' If she started to scream, I would kill her, I thought, and moved along the side of the bed and was right beside her. Then I put a knee up on the pillow, putting my right hand up and over her far shoulder and around under her chin. But her limpness and disregard for my actions began to affect me, and I hesitated. And then the thought came that her lack of resistance was part of her trickery, and that if I weakened she would laugh at me once again.

'I'll show you,' I said, and flattened my hands under her chin and thrust them down, under her own cold hands. As my fingers felt and took hold of her, she gasped, coming alive at last. She trembled violently as my palms rubbed over her, and she took ripping grabs at my wrists and she wrenched her body from side to side. I pulled both my knees hard against the small of her back and slid my hands up to grasp her shoulders, but at the instant of my loosening my grip she flung her legs about in a struggle of blankets and pushed herself up to her knees, her elbows swinging back frantically. I leaned to one side and thumped a forearm across her back, and, as she pitched forward, flung myself on top of her. My weight was pushing

185

her face downward into the bed; my chest was hard
against her back, and my face choking into her hair,
as I felt the bumping effort of her buttocks against
my thighs as she tried to free herself. I held her like
that for a moment, then slithered across her back and
rolled on my side against her, and her head lifted up,
straining her neck, as she gulped for air with stretching
lips, her eyes screwed shut. She had nearly smothered.
I kept my arm across her back, grasping her far
shoulder, tightening and relaxing the grip in rhythm
with her gasps. Then she dropped her head slowly
forward, her eyes still closed, until her forehead
touched the bed again, and not till then did I become
aware of the rasp of my own breath.

I waited for her, sure she was beaten. If she
screamed, that would be that. I did not care.

'You didn't think I would do it,' I said, lowering my
eyes to her shoulder and looking at the side of her face
through a mess of hair. Her lips were moist and slack.

'For God's sake,' she moaned, 'leave me alone.'

'I didn't want to hurt you,' I said.

She smacked the side of her hand against my ear
and twisted, her breath squealing. I had to fight her
again. Stretching out my arms, I took her by the
shoulders and, though she squirmed and kicked, had
only to pull her back and slide my arms around her
waist to beat her: I was so much stronger than she
was. She lashed about with her legs and swung her
elbows back again and again, so I ducked the side of
my face hard against the back of her head and
squeezed her in my grip, and waited. As her efforts
slackened I pulled her over on top of me and brought
my knees up around her hips and rolled her back again
in the grip of my legs. Then I forced her shoulders

around, keeping an arm under her neck and gripping her opposite arm, in the same movement trapping her near arm under my body. Scissored by my legs, her arms pinned, she might have been stretched on a rack. Turning slightly, I was able to prop myself up on the elbow under her head, and look down at her, with one hand free.

She was flushed with the effort of her struggle, and her eyes were glazed and rolling, and her lips were moving against each other, as though she was trying to talk without opening her mouth (I remembered), and the skin across the point of her chin, which was tilted up by the stretch of her neck against my arm, was in spasmodic movement in answer to involuntary contractions of her throat. And yet she was warm now and beneath the dull film of her eyes there glittered pin-points of light, and I was sure that as she looked up at me she did not believe I would do it. I reached down and pulled her pyjama top back, my hands brushing the firmness of her ribs, pushing against and then over the high mounds of her tautened body until they were bare to my eyes, and she moaned again, and her breath rose and fell, and her head rolled from side to side against her wild hair, and her stomach heaved in the grip of my legs, and below the spread fullness of deep flesh the rib-lines cut through her skin as she arched back across my knee. My own breath was so short that it was full in my mouth as I stared down at her. I dropped to my side again, turning my face on my arm and against her hair, my eyes shut, and, trying hard, brushed a hand over her damp-hot body and face. My hand became numb, unfeeling, but I kept it moving blindly over her, as my mind shuddered into the blackness of my eyes. Then I could not hold her. She wriggled and twisted away from me with a sudden wrench of her body and I started to sit up, trying to summon up the strength to make another fight of it.

I saw this blow coming, but was unable to duck it, and the side of my head took an awful thump. The sight of her wavered and then became fixed in slight pain again. This pain didn't worry me; I was getting used to being hit on the head. But I was finished, of course. She was sitting there, in furious colour, panting like billyho, the long hairbrush raised in her hand. I was half-raised on my elbow, all aggression gone, a lost cause if there ever was one. And then, rather to my surprise, she zonked me again on the head with this hairbrush. It seemed a little cold-blooded of her, but perhaps my defeat was not apparent; she was, after all, entitled to make sure of me.

'Give in,' I groaned, as everything flew into smithereens. 'I've had it.'

I wobbled up into a sitting position, blinking dazedly about at nothing in particular. As the fog cleared, I was surprised to feel a warm trickle down my cheeks. It was blood, of course, and I smeared the back of my hand across my cheeks, vaguely hoping that she would think that she had dished out enough punishment for my horrendous crimes. But when I looked at my hand there was nothing to see. And still my cheeks were streaming. In my mortification I could only sit there and suffer this tremendous humiliation: though there was no real emotion on my part, for I had been knocked cold and uncaring, my eyes were running amok and pouring out tears of their own accord.

Then I became conscious of her face quite close to

mine. 'Poor Robbie,' she said, and as I looked into the age and pallor of her face I knew she was seeing every rotten thing about me, even though my rottenness was finding no reflection in her eyes, or touching the strange skin of her strange face.

'It doesn't matter,' I said, dropping my head, the whole bundle, and kneeling across the bed to hide my disgusting tears in the pillow.

'Don't, Robbie,' she said. She would be sitting on the edge of the bed, looking down at me, recovered, knowing she had won. She did not have to be angry.

'It's all right,' she said.

I was crouched in the sand again, I knew; nothing had changed since that time on the beach: I was crouched in the sand, my face pressed in my hands, beaten, and she was looking down at me. Nothing had changed, or would change, because I was beaten once and for all.

After a while her hand brushed up my back to pat my head: the little boy would have to leave her room now.

'It's such a silly life,' she was saying.

Her whisper was nearer, and so strange that I felt compelled to turn my face and open my eyes.

This room was in darkness, and she was a warm shadow in this darkness whom I could sense but not see. The nearer, the warmer, a presence of mystery, she was leaning over me now and whispering.

Later on, she said, 'I'll stay with you for just a few more weeks, Robbie. It's not going to be such a bad sinking.'

9

I do not know what the real cost of the whole business was to Mrs Ranier. She stayed with me (and it was with me) for exactly two more weeks and then left. Our leave-taking was casual, considering what we had been up to, and in truth I felt casual; it seemed, in fact, that the time for her departure was in some subtle way chosen by me. And then she was gone, and for a while it was hard to believe in her existence, or really care about it. But from what she had said, I gathered that the idea of resuming her marriage did not appeal to her any longer.

'Goodbye, young Mr New Zealand,' were her last words to me, and there was no real pleasure in them, either.

Even this next morning after her going I was all right. Not that Harry Maddox noticed any difference; what was important was the difference I noticed. Harry came around late this Sunday morning and we stretched out in the backyard on the patch of lawn underneath the clothes-line. This lazy air Albertville carried the other six mornings of the week was now sanctified by church bells and some people, about one in twelve, say, had been up and about in their pious best in response to these bells. The blaze of green on the hills was fading, the lushness of the plateau lands exhausted, and the river clean and sparkling, the powdery silt mark of spring flooding high above its level now; the frown of the town's roofs was heating to the sun and the only noise to disturb this silence was the intermittent rumble of a lone tram for somebody who might want to go somewhere.

Harry had met a new girl at Raggleton Beach the previous afternoon, a Molly Sullivan, who was home on holiday from some Catholic convent in Wellington. He seemed to think he was breaking new ground in becoming acquainted with a girl of her denomination.

'She came into town and met me last night and I took her home after the pictures,' said Harry. 'She was dressed up to the nines and had a spot of high-powered scent tossed hither and yon, and I could see she was as keen as mustard on yours truly.'

'That's good,' I said, lolling back on my elbows and turning a blind face to the sun. I was feeling very tired.

'She's a great conversationalist is this Molly. I thought afterwards that I had told her practically everything I had done the last month, and a lot about myself, and she kept me going by making sensible observations.'

'Good on her.'

'And after the pictures, well, she really turned it on. I kissed her. She pretended to put up a little resistance. I mean I had to consider her pride. That was fair enough, the resistance, but then I got in a good long kiss and we were wooing for quite a while there.'

'Good on you,' I said.

'Girls are funny,' he went on. 'I mean I knew she wanted me to kiss her and she knew I knew, yet she pretended she didn't really, which is pretty funny.'

'That's the way they are,' I said. And yawned.

'How would you know?' said Harry. Amused, I turned my head away from the sun and watched him roll over on his back, his shirt and singlet a pillow for his head, and reach out with his arms as though the heat of the day was something he could embrace. This hair on his chest was becoming much denser and spreading up to his throat and about his stomach.

'Girls have a definite advantage when it comes to wooing,' he said now. 'I only thought of it last night on the way to the bus. They've got nothing to make them darned uncomfortable. They don't have worries like that at all.'

I sat up and pulled my shirt over my head. 'I think I'll get more sun, too,' I said.

'Girls have things to put up with we haven't,' said Harry. 'No doubt it's six of one and a half-dozen of the other.'

'Look, old chap,' I said wearily. 'Let's get off the subject – there are other things in life, y'know.'

'How would you know?' said Harry again, and laughed. I laughed, too.

But I do not know what the real cost of the whole business was to Mrs Ranier. I can only hope that every-thing turned out well for her, although I realise now that the odds might have been against that. At the time I didn't think of her as having anything at stake at all. I don't suppose I could have been expected to concern myself with her problems. I can do that now in retrospect, months later. There is nothing quite like being unselfish after the event. Anyway, she was lucky she did not get herself killed, I suppose.